SIMPLE GUIDE TO

THE HEBREW BIBLE

COVER ILLUSTRATION
One of the caves at Qumran where
the 'Dead Sea Scrolls' and fragments
of the Bible were found (p.109)

ABOUT THE AUTHOR
EDMUND HARTLEY originally intended to pursue a career in fine
arts, but after graduating from art school and completing two years
of National Service in the Army, he elected to train for the
priesthood and went to St John's Roman Catholic Seminary in
Surrey, England, where he joined two of his brothers. Later, he
returned to the Army, this time as a Chaplain, and served eighteen
years, including tours of duty in Germany, Northern Ireland and
Malaya. He is currently looking after a parish in south-east Kent,
and is the author of the *Simple Guide to The Roman Catholic Church*
in this World Religions series.

DRAWINGS BY IRENE SANDERSON
PHOTOGRAPHS BY HANAN ISACHAR

List of Illustrations

SIMPLE GUIDE TO

THE HEBREW BIBLE

EDMUND HARTLEY

GLOBAL BOOKS LTD

Simple Guides • Series 3
WORLD RELIGIONS

The Simple Guide to
THE HEBREW BIBLE
By Edmund Hartley

First published 2000 by
GLOBAL BOOKS LTD
PO Box 219, Folkestone, Kent CT20 3LZ

ISBN 1-86034-068-7

British Library Cataloguing in Publication Data
A CIP catalogue entry for this book
is available from the British Library

Set in Futura 10½ on 11½ point by Bookman, Hayes, Middlesex
Printed and bound in Malta by Interprint Ltd.

Contents

Biblical Map of the 'Near East'

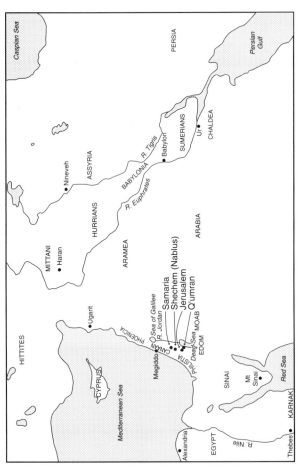

Foreword

My elderly couple, having at last found a smaller house and parted with much of the property for which they now had no room, were still loath to get rid of their books. Eventually, they decided that I should have them. I collected them in several boxes and installed a bookrack to hold them. As a family treasure, it was their prize collection; I promised to look after it. The old couple probably expected me to read them because I had showed an interest, but I wondered whether I would.

It had never occurred to my youthful mind that books were the end products of a great deal of work. First, someone has a thought then painstakingly writes it down whether in longhand or on a typewriter or PC; then comes the typesetting and page make-up, the printing, and finally the publishing and distribution/marketing! Only later did I realize that, in general, books are written to ask, or to answer contemporary questions; perhaps even to teach. Some people write deliberately for 'posterity' – and with a bit of luck, 'posterity' will read it, for a time, anyway!

All books, including fiction, are invariably about human nature, how it works and develops, including the 'discoveries' it makes along the way and about man's impact on the planet. Any other sort of literature just does not exist. And because the Books that we find in the Bible are no different, one of the initial aims of this *Guide* is to show how this particular group of Books came to be written, where the writers found their informatioin in the first place and what was probably in the minds of those responsible for their composition. We shall also discover what was original and what was not.

The author of *The Simple Guide to Judaism* in this series is such an author. He generously describes his work as a subjective exploration, rather than an objective study, of the texts and artefacts. He also feels that to '. . . appreciate a culture other than one's own is to make a conscious voyage of discovery – which attempts to understand the patterns which shape the lives of others'. This means keeping a mind that is open and prepared to take risks. It is with an eye on the outside influences that affected Judaism, that this *Guide* offers the sort of objective view that one would expect from an 'outsider' – but whose traditions, though also rooted in Judaism – have evolved differently. As a matter of interest, Jews, when speaking about their Sacred Writings, prefer the expression *'Tanach'* rather than 'Hebrew (or Jewish) Bible'.

'Hebrew' is not the only material to be found in the 'Bible' – a considerable amount of Greek material was added as this library was collected, developed and translated.

Libraries usually assist visitors by displaying their books under generic headings like 'Fiction', 'Non-Fiction', 'Science', 'Philosophy', 'Religion', 'Crime' etc. The Biblical writers, however, did not classify their books. This was not done until much later, when the Rabbis decided to organize this 'library'. If you know where to look, you will find elements of 'Fiction', 'History', 'Poetry', 'Genealogies', 'Meditations' and even 'Crime' throughout the Bible.

Even before there was such a thing as 'writing', people were sharing ideas. Eventually, over a very long time, and only after 'writing' had been discovered, were their attempts to express and record their ideas gathered into some sort of order. The collection of the resulting 'Books' is what you have in your hands when you pick up a Bible; of course, now it is very convenient to have this collection all under one cover.

□

In finding out why, how and when this 'Bible' Collection was put together, I realized, that some of the ideas I had been taught had been treasured for centuries but were not as accurate as I had been led to believe.

While there is nothing the matter with 'old wives' tales', which can serve a purpose and be very positive, one cannot help questioning such 'tales' when they are preferred to scientific explanations. Besides, many people have their own favourite Biblical passages and would consider it impertinent for anyone to question the value of such treasures. Even so, 'traditionalists' may be pleasantly surprised to find that, without offending too many sensibilities, some of these inaccurate notions can be rectified quite easily without causing too much distress.

Guides do not normally operate from an armchair. So, once engaged, your guide will escort you round and point out places of interest and perhaps answer some questions. So you ought first to have 'arrived' at a Bible containing both the Old and the New Testaments. Your companion – that's me – can now point out places of interest and provide you with some of the background.

The Bible is Completed c135 AD

The 'Hebrew Bible', including the New Testament, which actually contains Aramaic and Greek material, is said to have been completed during the second century AD. Since then, it has remained largely unchanged. Though a lot of non-Hebrew material was added earlier, no additions seem to have appeared since about 135AD, (apart from the mistakes made by copyists). Recently, however, footnotes have begun to accumulate on each page. Though the New Testament is partly written in Hebrew, it is not generally accepted as part of the religious history of the Hebrew people.

'Hebrews', 'Israelites' and 'Jews'

The 'Hebrews', an ancient nation, were later known as 'Israelites' for centuries until about 587BC when the Babylonians destroyed their kingdom known as 'Judah' and decided that, henceforth, they be called 'Jews'. This was not to apply to the Samaritans (p.62), who, because of their infidelity to the Pact (Covenant) were considered by the Hebrews to be 'non-Jew'.

1

Discovering What the Bible Is

Plants that thrived in Biblical times. From left to right:
pomegranate, papyrus or bulrush, lily, acacia

THE CONVENTIONAL VIEW

Casual visitors to the old castle are told who built it,
when and what its purpose was and whether there
were any major events connected with it. The oldest
elements of the building stand out clearly. Any
subsequent additions, usually in a later style of

architecture are shown in the brochure. Following the same idea, visitors to the Bible find a continual story unfolding when we start reading it from the beginning.

The conventional understanding of the Bible is that everything begins with the account of Creation – in the Book of GENESIS, which contains the first appearance of people – our first parents who are called 'Adam and Eve'. They are punished for breaking a taboo – a punishment in which all their descendants are to share. Their children, named Cain and Abel, fall out – Abel dies at the hands of his jealous brother, who then gets marked with the 'sign of Cain'. This heralds the troubles that bring about the Flood, which only Noah, his family and the animals survive.

After the Tower of Babel story, Abraham, a nomadic shepherd, wanders in from the Chaldea (Persian Gulf). He later appears as a military genius. God makes a Promise (Covenant or Pact) to Abraham that he is to be the head of a great nation, a Promise that gets repeated to each of his descendants, Ishmael, Isaac and Jacob. Abraham's slave girl, Hagar, bears him a son, Ishmael, from whom the religion of Islam is said to have arisen. Sodom and Gomorrah get destroyed, because they are evil places. Then Abraham's wife, Sarah, gives birth to Isaac. The story of Joseph, one of Jacob's sons, who is sold into slavery in Egypt, brings Genesis to a close.

'THE LAW' DEFINES THE JEWISH TRADITION

EXODUS tells of Moses and the great escape from Egypt, which includes the giving of the Law ... the

Capernaum, a frieze of the Covenant found in the third-century synagogue

Ten Commandments. Then come the Books of
LEVITICUS, NUMBERS and DEUTERONOMY which expand
and explain the Law. The Law now becomes *the*
condition that had to be honoured if the people were
to benefit from the Promise made to Abraham.

The earliest traditions recognized Genesis and
these Books of the Law as the written work of Moses.
In turn, Christendom also accepted this as fact,
particularly because the Christ spoke of Moses as
their author.

Under Joshua, the Egyptian escapees invade
Canaan and, with the assistance of a number of
heroes (JUDGES), conquer the country. The Books of
SAMUEL, KINGS and CHRONICLES tell how David then
settled their New Kingdom. This Kingdom broke into
two after the death of his son, Solomon, and
eventually collapsed under pressure from neighbour-
ing empire-builders.

What followed was a general falling off of
religious fervour. The Prophets then insisted that
'keeping the Law' was the guarantee of their survival;
but the people would not listen. The Books of PSALMS,
JOB, DANIEL, together with the SONG OF SONGS, all
played an important part in the unfolding of this part
of the story. But, for the Hebrews, their Escape from
Egyptian slavery plus the giving of the Commandments that comprised the Law of God, were the most
important events. As already noted, it was the Law
that made their Scriptures so important to them. It was
not until the Maccabean Revolt (c165BC) that a new
development takes place – when Jews were now
prepared to die for their religion.

The next notable event was the coming of the Christ. His Birth, Death, Resurrection and Ascension were to be related in the 'GOSPELS' of the New Testament. The Gospels are then followed with some directions that were composed as 'LETTERS'. Later developments (ACTS OF THE APOSTLES) and a long series of meditations (REVELATIONS) complete the last part of the Biblical Library. Even though it has moved far beyond the Jewish tradition, Christendom generally regards the Bible as the 'Word of God'.

ANOTHER PERSPECTIVE

As we cherish the tradition reflected in that ancient castle, we cherish and respect the Bible because it is also part of our heritage. The completed castle stands there, while successive generations maintain it, preventing it becoming a ruin. The Bible, too, is complete – in the sense that nothing has been added to it for nearly 2,000 years. As it is for the Jews, the Bible is also Christendom's 'Holy Book'. Biblical rituals are still used extensively by both religious systems, as they reflect past usage – just as the Biblical stories reflect even earlier events. Like the castle built on a hill, it is kept 'alive', not only by constant visits and the memories of past guided tours, but also by archaeological research.

Because it was thought to be too dangerous, it was not until recently that anyone felt like looking at the foundations to find out what was there *before* the castle. Since archaeologists dig up evidence to answer such questions, there must also be evidence that applies to ancient writings. What was there *before* the Bible? Neither the castle nor the Bible just fell out of the sky!

But unlike the castle, the oldest parts of the Bible are not quite so clear-cut; and just a casual examination will reveal little about its foundations. The Bible actually begins where you would least expect it. Truth to tell, the stories we find in it sound more like human stories that describe human ideas in human language. The human language, used in the composition of the Bible, reveals the changing and developing mindset of its writers, just as one would expect over such a long period of over a thousand years.

□

Over the past two thousand years, the Hebrew Bible has been accepted as the unique account of what one race of people gave as the reason for its existence and its destiny. While it is largely about the development of a particular type of human culture, and contains 'God's Law', it is only from about the fourth century AD, that the Bible as a whole came to be described as 'The Word of God'.

At the time of writing, however, the authors were not unanimous about this! It is unfortunate, that, while it was being put together, no one thought it necessary to produce a separate handbook giving a résumé of its contents. It would have been a great advantage, for instance, to know how much of man's 'history' had been left out of the Bible; and then to have been given an explanation for some of the more obscure passages, or 'how it all should be understood'. It is because there are no explanations, many people down the ages have thought the Bible to be 'self-explanatory'.

However, the suggestion that 'handbooks might have been useful' is not so outlandish after all. Such 'explanations' are actually to be found in the *Mishnah, Midrash* and *Targums*. These are separate collections of traditional pious interpretations, which, along with the legends, were handed down by word of mouth. In order to help the memory and also to preserve them, eventually they got written down – many being incorporated in the Biblical texts. This was done from about the second century BC onwards, and on into the Christian era.

SUMMARY

So we need to know which parts of the Bible are actually the 'Word of God', and which are pious reflections; and then in what *sense* they are to be understood as the 'Word of God'. It is important to know how much is the 'Word of God' and how much of it is solely man's contribution. (See Chapters 8 and 9.) As we go on, it will become clearer that there is much more to the Bible than meets the eye.

Both approaches have been developed over the centuries and have become quite sophisticated. But they both treat the Bible as an historical novel, which in places requires explanation. The Bible is actually an unsophisticated collection of 'theological' works strung together by primitive Jewish thinkers, using narratives, which, occasionally, can be verified from secular sources. The 'conventional view', being more literal, does not take account of such considerations.

Bedouins in the Sinai desert

2

Primitive Beginnings

Clay cult figures (150mm high) of fertility goddess Astarte.
Eighth century BC, found in coastal area inhabited by
Philistines

WHAT IS CIVILIZATION?

Some knowledge of the past shows us that 'civiliza-tion' is a developing experience. This guided tour joins it in the twenty-first century, when, compared with the past, it looks arguably better. Those familiar with 'evolution' see it continuing to evolve. While many think it is only a theory, some aspects of evolution are plain to see. It is now generally accepted that man has been around for over 400,000 years, but most agree that Homo Sapiens did not start 'civilized'. Though evidence for anything that could be described as 'intelligent' does not go back much beyond then (see p.49), it would suggest, at least, that evolution has still some way to go. Indeed, were the notion of 'evolution' to be shown to be a fact of life, no one could be expected to believe that 'evolution' is now complete.

We do not know and therefore cannot imagine, what life would have been like before such a process began – before, say, 'writing' had been invented. What was it like when there were no 'numbers' – or when there is no such thing as 'reading'?

Primitive man would, of course, be aware of 'daytime' and the fact that you cannot see well at 'night' – but again, it would take millennia before there was any general consensus that the sun had anything to do with this. People might have talked about it – and eventually began to wonder. But it is in the 'wondering', with fresh information in hand, that our *Simple Guide* begins. This Guide is concerned with a collection of Books that contain material, the origins of which are shrouded in the mists of prehistory.

'Civilization' transforms what has gone before and with it comes the burgeoning of 'scientific knowledge', mathematics, physics, etc. and, after another mere 20,000 years, in the industrialized world at any rate, electronics. Our guided tour starts from a time when there is no knowledge of anything apart from the simplest things: day and night, hot and cold, life and death and the habits of prey; and how to make weapons and, later, tools.

WHEN DID CIVILIZATION FIRST APPEAR?

We are concerned here, however, with the Near

East, where modern civilization was developing some 10,000 years ago. In its southern extremity, along the Nile Valley, Egypt was becoming important, with its kings and dynasties. In the north, Asia Minor was the home of the Hittites, an equally powerful people. To the east, in Mesopotamia, where the Rivers Tigris and Euphrates provided a very fertile area, arose the magnificent civilization of the Akkadians and the Babylonians, along with the Sumerians, who produced the first writing. Close by, the Assyrian empire was also beginning to grow. Further to the east were the Medes and Persians (present-day Iraq and Iran). Between them and squeezed up against the Mediterranean seaboard was Canaan – Canaan is the area, which will interest us most.

Later on, other peoples came from the west – first the Greeks and then the Romans. They would come to occupy all these areas. It was during the Roman occupation, and up to about 170 AD that the last material found in the Bible was to be collected.

Having compared this writing with other contemporary material, we can now provide fairly accurate dates for the composition of the different 'books' in our Biblical Library. Those responsible for their composition lived in Canaan and were clearly affected by their geographic location. The mountain range to the east of the Jordan separated them from the desert beyond, while they occupied an area of fertile land, which lay across the main trade routes. People to the south, north, east and west, all in their turn, overran Canaan, or 'Palestine' as the Greeks later called it. It was an attractive country and was clearly important for economic reasons.

THE EGYPTIAN VIEW OF THE WORLD

Those who enjoy travelling are often amazed that people living in dry and sunny climates usually appear to be naturally optimistic despite their immediate situations. Such were the Egyptians, with their predictable seasons. The Egyptians came to worship gods that were regarded as heavenly benefactors who looked after their people and generally blessed them with a sunny disposition.

Over thousands of years, the Egyptians developed legends covering the exploits of over seven hundred such gods. Amongst themselves, the Egyptian family of gods were said to enjoy good relations. Their chief god, initially Aten, (Horus) the sun-god, caused everyone much anxiety when he disappeared each evening; but, after vanquishing Apep and all the reptile spirits of the night, this anxiety evaporated with the light of dawn.

A hymn to this sun-god, written by the Pharaoh, Akenaten about 1250BC, may well have been the inspiration for Psalm 104 (Book of Psalms) which was written between 500-400BC. This Aten, later called Amon, (Amon-Ra), had engineered the Creation of the world through an act of solitary sexual relief. Once a year, the Pharaoh, later seen as the 'embodiment' of Amon, would come to Karnak, the huge Temple on the banks of the Nile, to perform a similar rite, recalling the act of creation, and to receive a blessing for so doing.

The Egyptians taught that Man and the animal kingdom had all arisen from the mud of the Nile and, at death, would all receive a place in a 'never-never' world full of material benefits. To ensure this, the burial chambers of the rich were crammed with every conceivable necessity.

In Egypt, Amon-Ra had arranged the massacre of those who were unfaithful to him, but in contrast to the Mesopotamian legends, his 'goodness' prevented him from permitting the extermination of the entire human race. However, apart from the myth of Osiris, the greatest in the Egyptian pantheon of gods, comparatively little detailed Egyptian mythology has survived. While some of it can be learnt from hieroglyphics in the pyramids and temples, most of what we know comes from Plutarch, a Greek. He did not appear until much later, when the Egyptian legends were already 2,500 years old. Homer did the same for the ancient Greek legends.

THE MESOPOTAMIAN VIEW OF THE WORLD

In contrast with the people of Egypt, where the convenient Nile flooded at set times, those living in Mesopotamia had a generally pessimistic view of life. The reason suggested for this is the unpredictable flooding of the threatening Tigris and Euphrates rivers. Archaeologists have found evidence of the extensive damage caused by their inundations. Storms accompanied by torrential rainfall produced the notion that their gods were equally unpredictable, capricious and always squabbling among themselves.

Complaining of all they had to do to maintain the Cosmos, these gods conspired to create Mankind to look after it instead. So Man was created to be a 'slave' on whom the gods then worked out their frustrations. Man's destiny was to resign himself to try (in vain) to please his gods – who nonetheless sentenced him to death, after which there was nothing but a 'never-never' sad and shadowy existence.

We have the benefit of the *Gilgamesh* (see p.42) and the *Atrahasis* epics which provide this insight. A copy of the Atrahasis epic, dating from about 1600BC, tells how their chief god 'Marduk' made mankind from earth mixed with the blood of the murdered god, 'Kingu'. Unfortunately for this human race of 'slaves', Man 'multiplied and caused trouble', so the gods tormented him with a series of 'punishments' which culminated in a total flood. However, a hero, called 'Utanapishtim', secretly warned of the impending danger by the god 'Ea', then escaped with his family by boat – accompanied by a pair of 'every animal in existence'.

His escape caused great irritation to reverberate among the gods, because there were not supposed to have been any survivors. It also provides some explanation for the Mesopotamian peoples' pessimistic and fatalistic approach to life. Those Hebrews who were exiled to Assyria and Babylon between 721 and 538 BC, will have learnt such stories and chosen some of them when relating *their* own pre-history, in the book of Genesis.

Interestingly enough, archaeologists have recently discovered some evidence for a catastrophic flood in the area of the Black Sea, and have dated their findings to around 5,000BC.

THE INVENTION OF 'WRITING'

About 3,200 BC, the Sumerians, living in south-eastern Mesopotamia, invented 'writing'. In Egypt, the hieroglyphics, a picture writing technique, was later replaced with a simplified, 'demotic', script about 1800BC. It is not known whether this was familiar to the Habiru (see Ch.3), but they may have learnt Sumerian writing before adopting the Aramaean method. (The Chinese had already produced the ideogram, which, though unrelated, had a pattern of strokes similar, in some ways, to that of the Sumerian cuneiform script.)

The Sumerian script is 2,500 years older than the Roman alphabet currently in use in the West. An early example of this can be seen on Trajan's Doric Column in Rome (built 106-113AD). We also have fragments of a Sumerian version of the Biblical 'Babel' Story (Book of Genesis Ch.11). This Sumerian version dates from as far back as the Third Dynasty of Ur (2,065-1,060BC) and fragments of it are now in Oxford's Ashmolean Museum. It is a story that tells of two rival Babylonian gods 'Enki' and 'Enlil'. Out of spite, they put an end to the common language that man was always said to share with the gods, by creating new languages, thus confusing and separating them.

MAN'S 'NEED' FOR THE GODS

The constant squabbling between 'peoples-on-the-ground' began to be seen as a reflection of this rivalry among these 'gods-in-the-clouds'. (The Book of Genesis reflects this idea by first showing Man in

conversation with God in a relationship that eventually breaks down.) In those far-off days every
'earthly happening' was taken to be a reflection of
what took place in the clouds. It was an idea, which,
perhaps coincidentally, eventually formed the basis
of the system taught by the Greek philosopher, Plato,
in the fifth century BC.

With the continued absence of any evidence to
the contrary, we find that Man, over great stretches
of time, gradually devises his own gods to which he
then binds himself through various rituals – rituals
which effectively begin to increase his religious
subservience. Human sacrifice, common to many
primitive religious systems, eventually completes the
circle in which Man enslaves himself to his gods.

You might well say that this last observation shows
'hindsight' at work, since that was certainly not the
way in which our ancestors felt about their 'truths'
and religious rituals. Such rituals were arguably as
important to them then, as our own religious rites are
to us today. The Egyptian and then the Mesopotamian notions had lasting effects in the Near East,
particularly the Canaanite understanding of things. It
is this Canaanite understanding that is featured in the
composition of the Biblical Books and what makes
them unique.

In 1929, archaeologists working at Ugarit (present-day's Ras Shamra, in Syria) discovered manuscripts dating from about 1,500BC, which give us a
lot more information about the climate of affairs as it
was in the Near East at the time of Abraham – about
2,000BC, the first significant character to appear in
the Bible (Genesis. Ch.11).

3

Who Were the Hebrews?

Shrine of the Book, Jerusalem, which houses the Dead Sea Scrolls

THE HABIRU

The word 'Habiru' was originally an Egyptian term for a particular social class of people, chiefly 'outsiders', which had gradually appeared in Egypt during the third millennium BC. By 2,000BC we find the word 'Habiru' being used for people who appeared to be 'foreign elements', or 'prisoners of war eligible for ransom'; later it included 'mercenaries'. 'Enemy marauders' were even described as 'Habiru': in Arabic the word is 'Barrani'.

Hammurabi, who ruled the Amorite dynasty 1728-1686BC, numbered 'Habiru' among his royal body-guard. In the cuneiform tablets of the fifteenth-fourteenth centuryBC (known as the 'Armana Letters') we find reference to 'Habiru' volunteering for slavery to better their economic lot. (A thousand years later, this was commonplace among those living beyond the boundaries of the Roman Empire.)

As time goes by, 'Habiru', wherever they were found, continue to be seen as 'foreigners', or 'outlanders'. As such they never seem to belong to one particular ethnic group. For the Egyptians, Habiru were 'foreigners' wherever they came from! There-fore it would not be correct to say that all 'Habiru' were Semites, nor would it be correct to think that they all originally shared the same language. They would use the local spoken language in whatever settled areas they infiltrated.

Canaanites, then, who were suffering famine, joined the 'Hittites' as they migrated to Egypt from the north. Here, all were classed as 'Habiru'; a modern equivalent for them being 'economic or political refugees'.

THE 'HEBREWS' APPEAR

After having settled in Egypt for about 'four hundred' years, [1] some of the Habiru migrated north again. This was to become a particular 'race of people' called 'Hebrews'. They begin to emerge at

---

1. 'four hundred years' is suggested in Genesis 15:23 and Acts 7:6

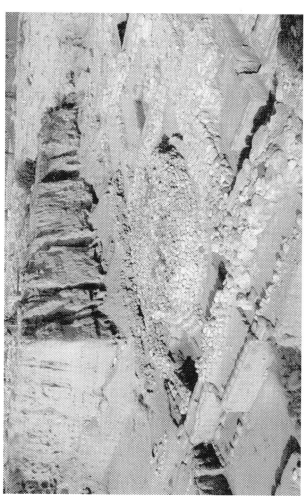

Historic altar at the tenth-century BC Israelite city of Megiddo

the beginning of the first millennium BC, when we find a great 'palaver' taking place at 'Sichem' in Palestine. Also known as Sichar, (the site of Jacob's Well), it was a town of great strategic importance; it still exists, with its updated name, 'Nablus'.

This meeting of the various groups of Habiru immigrants North from Egypt and now integrating with the indigenous population, aimed at consolidating their occupation of what is known as Palestine, and 'Hebrew' begins to appear as a spoken language – but not for long. The Aramaic language, the script of which seems to have been used for writing Hebrew, soon overtook spoken Hebrew.

WHAT LANGUAGES WERE USED?

By 2,000BC Aramaic had become the international language throughout much of the Near East. With the rise of Phillip of Macedonia (382-336BC) and his son Alexander the Great (356-323BC) came the spread of a new art and learning. The Greek 'koine', or 'common' language, then replaced Aramaic, and for the next 500 years Greek was the commercial language of the Eastern Mediterranean.

Greek was the language into which the Hebrew Scriptures were first translated, and the language in which much of the New Testament was composed. Before the turn of the fourth century AD, the Latin spoken in the Roman Empire, which stretched from the Middle East to Britain, had become the language of preferment.

Later still, French became the international language throughout Europe and, eventually, English, as it is today. The Near East retained the Greek, Armenian, Syriac and Coptic languages for Church rituals for well over 1000 years, while Europe, and more recently the Americas, the East and the Far East, used Latin in its religious rituals. However, in the 1960s, the Latin used in Western Church services was replaced by the 'vernacular' (the language used for local day-to-day business in whatever country).[2]

By now (beginning of the twenty-first century), people generally have lost the sense and the sound of Latin. In the same way, though the Hebrew language was used in their Temple Liturgy, the Hebrews used Aramaic in their day-to-day exchanges, so that by the end of the Old Testament period they would have had little recollection of Hebrew as their common language. In Israel, it is again the language of daily speech.

SUMMARY

Over a period of some 40,000 years of living with nature, Man's basic needs begin to be identified and rules, ordered towards the good of the community, start to emerge.

For primitive people, living from hand-to-mouth, and having no real understanding of 'future', everything of importance seems to come from the past. So

---

2. The Apostolic religious rituals found in the New Testament were conducted in Greek until Byzantine traditions took root, by which time the West was already using Latin. These two traditions have been developing separately ever since.

the old folk are no longer killed off, but begin to be honoured for their experience. The 'past' then gets built into the tradition that shapes their evolving ideas. Taboos develop and become the rules by which people live. Notions of gods appear in support of these taboos and, with the passage of time, these all grow together.

This is what provides later generations with the material that they will absorb as 'true' because it has 'always been so'. It is an easily recognizable evolutionary process. Like the river, following the line of least resistance, eventually, becomes the 'obvious reality'. Different groups of peoples commit to writing their understanding of things, using traditional material to give validity to their compositions.

But the Bible is different from other ancient sagas, not only that, by comparison, it is relatively recent, but we can now see that the writers and compilers, without being aware of it, were involved in a *theological* exercise. Their work is centred on a single god who had given them a reason for being. They used geography, history, economics and politics but only in so far as these could be shown to explain their particular relationship with God. Theirs was a unique way of looking at reality – but it was *their* way, not ours. We were to come later.

4

Abraham and Canaan

Third century AD fresco showing two of twelve tribesmen who escaped with Moses from Egypt. Found on the wall of a synagogue in Syria

We first meet Abraham with his relatives, in Genesis (11:27). They were Terahites and, among other gods, they worshipped the Moon. Their original homeland is thought to be Chaldea, but they probably started their trip to Canaan from northern Mesopotamia, from its main town, Haran, from where Abraham began the second leg of his journey. (As it is quite a hike from what is now called Kuwait to what is now called Jerusalem, a much shorter journey is suggested in line with the journeys undertaken by other characters who feature in secular annals of the time.)

Megiddo – ruins from the time of King Solomon

Abraham's journey was part of an Amorite migration, which lasted several generations and involved settlements all over the Near East. In the same way, Joseph's trip in Egypt is part of the Hittite migration (1720-1570BC). Joseph became one of the 'Hyksos' – 'Hyksos' being the Egyptian word for 'foreign rulers'.

Discoveries in the 1960s and 70s made by Italian archaeologists at ancient Ebla (the modern Tell Mardikh, south of Aleppo, in northern Syria) have revealed the existence of a western Semitic empire of extensive commercial and cultural influence. Though, curiously, this has left hardly a trace, no less than 20,000 clay tablets have been found there. These mention some patriarchal names like Eber, Abraham, Ishmael, Israel, and Esau, along with other geographical and tribal names that are also found in Genesis and in other parts of the Bible.

THE NAME OF 'GOD'

What is even more interesting is that these tablets provide evidence of a 'god' that is invoked under the name 'Yah' or 'Ya'u'. It will not require much imagination to see this name as the first Hebrew attempt to give a name to *their* God. It is therefore probable that the name 'YAH-WEH' was known long before it was revealed to Moses on Mount Sinai.

As we thumb through the early Books of the Old Testament, we should not to be surprised to find that, originally, the Hebrew God had many different names. Some of them are still listed in Psalm 91. Abraham, the first individually named 'outsider' that we come across, became a Canaanite and, eventually, a very influential personage in the development of the history of the Canaanite people as recorded in the Book of Genesis (Ch.11 onwards). It is worth noting that the chief god in Canaanite mythology, called 'El', was shown in the form of a bull. Later, we meet this god – known as the 'golden calf' – in the desert story in the Book of Exodus.

The Habiru Choice of Gods

Religious people today might be upset to discover that as the Habiru picked up their languages, they also got the names for their gods from their host countries. Genesis tells us that their chief god's name was 'Elohim' who headed the 'Elim' (the group name for the Canaanite gods).

Inter-tribal squabbling probably resulted in the Canaanites having to arrange the resignation of the benign 'El' as head of their family of gods. They replaced 'El' with 'Baal', the equivalent of the Mesopotamian storm god. Baal's sister, 'Astarte' (goddess of war) and 'Mot', the god of death were among others.

For the previous four hundred years, the Habiru people had enjoyed the optimistic mindset of the Egyptians and shared their religion. Migrating north again, in the twelfth-eleventh centuries BC, meant inevitably their integration with the indigenous Canaanites. Emerging as a nation that became known as the 'Hebrews', they settled along the West Bank of the Jordan. By then, they had begun to worship 'Yahweh' as their god. [*The Simple Guide to Judaism* has further information on the sacred name – 'YHWH'.]

The different names the Hebrews gave to this god were taken from other contemporary religions and can be found in all the early copies of the Old Testament Books. (To avoid the later confusion, many of these names were translated out.)

THE CANAANITE MIND-SET

The Habiru people that settled in Egypt, is the subject of Exodus. Like all those Hittite Habiru, they had been infused with the benign Egyptian culture. Now they were to be confused by the pessimistic mind-set of the Canaanite people, the original natives who still occupied the area. It is with these people that the returning immigrants began to reintegrate. Generally speaking, religious confusion does not last long, and the Habiru were easily attracted by the Canaanite religion, not so much by its capricious gods but by its openly sensual rituals.

In order to find out how those far-off people thought about the beginning of things in the Near East during the Bronze Ages, let us now look in some detail at the way primitive people begin to 'reason' about these things.

5

The Myth Factor

Detail of 1800BC wall painting showing bull being led to ritual slaughter by Semitic tribesman. Found at palace at Mari on river Euphrates, Mesopotamia

WHAT IS MEANT BY 'MYTH'?

All civilizations, initially, rejoiced in extensive mythologies. Our interest here lies in those mythologies of the Near East which, fortunately for us, have now been largely recovered. Since the discovery (in 1929) of surviving documents of ancient Ugaritic languages (see p.28), we have been given a partial insight into the thinking of the people who lived in Mesopotamia 4,000 years ago. Among these is the mythical epic of *Gilgamesh* (see p.26), which, beyond doubt, is the most famous literature of ancient Mesopotamia.

But mention the word 'myth', and immediately you are likely to hear the patronizing reaction: 'I know – another 'fairy story'! It is worth remembering that the word 'myth' is a technical expression. Students of ancient cultures – in which 'myth' plays an important part, are well acquainted with its meaning.

Our ancient ancestors only had their senses to tell them of the nature of the Cosmos. When they got round to bringing reason to bear on what they could see, hear and feel, they produced what are now called 'myths'. With this device they accounted for the strange cosmic happenings over which they had no control. It would be a few thousand years before it was discovered that rain does not come through the holes normally occupied by the stars . . . and another thousand years before anyone realized that lightning was a flash of static electricity rather than an army of gods engaged in a brawl. (When I was little, I was told that 'thunder' was God being angry with me for being naughty. Terrifying!)

It may take another thousand years to discover that good and evil are not the result of divine caprice, but rather the way in which we describe things. Even so, though perhaps in jest, we still occasionally justify the existence of goodness, as well as the misery we experience, as an expression of God's capricious whimsy. One is unlikely to forget General Patton, who, when in the Ardennes in 1944, sought to promote his Chaplain, for 'arranging good weather' by composing a prayer for him – that actually worked!

Generally speaking, 'myth' is couched in the form of a story. But the story that 'myth' tells is not historical – it was not intended to be. Though they had a sense of the past, those far-off people had no sense of 'history' – in today's sense of the word. 'Myth' merely explains, in primitive language, the 'way things are'. Therefore, the event which is portrayed in this primitive manner will not be the 'singular event in the past', but a recurring event which happens in the 'timeless Now'. This is why it never loses its validity; and why all its characters belong both to the past and to the present. You will not find any dates for the 'Gilgamesh story'!

Primitive minds would not be aware of 'myth' in the sense, or the terms in which it is defined here. For them 'myth' was a matter of common sense! By the time 'myths' reach the form in which we discover them, they were already mixtures of stories which were themselves the result of generations of previous ideas about the development of the Cosmos. ('Universe' is, of course, a relatively modern term.)

The Gilgamesh Epic

The Babylonian Gilgamesh epic, already developing for over 1,000 years, was known not only to the Hittite people who lived in the North, but also in Palestine. Briefly, this was a poem in twelve cantos telling of a Sumerian hero, Gilgamesh, whose personal pride in his exploits aggravated his gods. Impatient with his arrogance, the gods produced a monster, 'Enkidu', to cut him down to size. However, a woman seduces Enkidu thereby changing him into human form.

The modern fable 'Beauty and the Beast' is partly an echo of this ancient legend. Enkidu then makes friends with Gilgamesh and together they accomplish many daring exploits. When Enkidu dies, Gilgamesh becomes terrified at the prospect of his own death, and sets himself to find immortality. He meets 'Utanapishtim' (who had escaped the Flood) who tells him of the secret of the 'herb of life'. Gilgamesh eventually finds it – only to have it stolen from him by a snake. Gilgamesh is thus forced sadly to accept death as inevitable.

The whole of this story, and the epic of Atrahasis, are both clearly pessimistic in their portrayal of reality, and are quite different from what we know of the optimistic Egyptian stories. While we now have the Biblical Creation stories to hand, it is a simple matter to compare them with these Mesopotamian epics which had already been assimilated into ancient Canaanite mythological thinking. It is this that then gets reflected in Hebrew religious thinking as it developed later in Palestine.

Though people nowadays may not be familiar with the details of Greek, Norse and Roman myths, at least they know *about* them. There are also Buddhist and Hindu myths; as well as Egyptian and Hebrew attempts to explain the Cosmos.

Myths appear very distorted to us today because we have all been brought up in a scientific age. But we need some assistance to recognize this 'distortion' for what it is. The distortion we find in the myth is not due to the mythology itself, but to the way in which the reality (of which the myth is the reflection) is observed. For instance, the scientist reckons his calculations are correct – he has already checked them rigorously. However, his conclusions, if eventually found to be incorrect – are only wrong, *not* because he made a mistake in his calculations but because someone has since discovered a distortion in the material on which he was working. (One clear example of 'mythical' thinking is the way in which the 'creation of Light' is separated from the later 'creation of the Sun – to guard the day' can be seen in the Book of Genesis Ch.1).

Those who would debunk myths as 'irrational dreams', usually measure them against their own standards of reasoning and will obviously find 'myth' wanting. But those people with comparatively unscientific cultures had only mythological 'thinking' with which to explain those situations or circum-stances. We know now that the earth has been a sphere for over 6000m years. But this fact was not generally accepted in Europe until only about 700 years ago. It was only 350 years ago that it was realized, but not generally accepted, that the earth orbits the sun and not vice versa!

Myth 'Logic'

What we now call 'myth', was, for the ancients, *the obvious explanation of things* in the 'common sense' of the time. For example: if a particular day has to be extended so that a victory can be won in a battle, the easiest way is to show that the sun stood still and to have got one of their gods to fix it! (Book of Joshua 10:10ff)

'MYTH' – A PRACTICAL EXAMPLE

In practical terms, 'myth' works like this:

'Myth' first takes a great question and turns it into a

'day-to-day' story. This day-to-day story is then projected into an imaginary world . . . (a world that does not yet exist) . . . the gods (who eventually get constructed to run this imaginary world) are then persuaded to provide the reason behind the story. And it is *this*, which eventually gets believed! Over the generations the fact that their forebears originated the story gets forgotten; because, by then, the gods will have 'minds of their own' and new generations of people have to follow them. People then have to imitate these gods in order to get them to do what they want.

'If the gods are fertile, our soil and our flocks will also be fertile. If not – disaster will surely follow'. We do not really know how much time it takes for such ideas to evolve, but we know that these gods were, originally, 'imaginary realities' (which people had made for themselves). Having established their existence, man then satisfies himself by worshipping them as having an existence of their own.

So it was necessary for the ancients to compel their gods to be fertile. In the light of the importance of their own survival, the aim of all ancient religious rites was to force the gods to come together in intercourse. For this reason, union with the temple prostitutes, in Babylon or the high places of Canaan, was not the orgy one might have imagined, but a religious rite aimed at securing the fertility of the soil, the livestock and their womenfolk.

The Egyptian temple in Tinmah (Israel)

Why the Namibian Bushmen Survive

Even today the extraordinary inhabitants of the Namibian desert, live as they have lived for centuries. They have existed in an environment so harsh and unyielding, that, by most human standards, is uninhabitable. Yet the bushmen living there, survive by combining an understanding of both nature and the surrounding wildlife with a knowledge of their ancestral lore.

'Myth', therefore, was the common mind-set – the 'common sense' of the time. So, despite all the national differences in speech and forms of expression, we can now understand why the early Bible Books should use 'myth' as a language.

HOW THE BIBLICAL WRITERS WERE INSPIRED

However, the Biblical writers were to transform this language profoundly as we see one 'idea' being imposed on another. In composing their Creation stories, the Biblical writers were clearly inspired by these great myths. But by the time they began to write, they would have begun to 'rethink' these myths in a way that would serve to promote their burgeoning belief in a single God. We need to remember that myth speaks of the existence of imaginary persons that exist outside time and therefore do *not* enter human history.

The 'Bible' begins to part company with 'myth' when its first readers were able to accept the then more developed Hebrew idea, namely, that their God is real, one alone, who actually *does* enter into human affairs. This was a new notion and clearly

unique; and, when we look at the materials those
writers used, we will find further reasons for
recognizinttempts to re-write, for example Books are
from all· other contemporary literature.

SUMMARY

By the time any writing gets done, all that anyone
'knew' about the past was in terms of myth and
legend; the myth and legend, originating in Egypt
and Mesopotamia, were already firmly fixed in the
Hebrew mind. It is from this wealth of tradition, that
the writers, who composed their Hebrew origins,
would select their stories. Though they were aware of
the past, they had no 'history' in any modern sense.
Even so, each writer had a different agenda and
would use those past traditions to suit his purpose.
This would prove a headache for those who later
came to edit and compile the 'books'!

But by the time later editors got their hands on
them, they had themselves acquired an updated
agenda and were looking for contemporary material
that would mean something to the readers of *their*
time. [There is always a temptation to employ a fresh
approach, as is seen in recent attempts to re-write,
for example, the Lord's Prayer.]

We can be sure, by now, that the sequence of the
various Books in our Biblical Library, are not as they
were initially composed; nor were they in any sort of
order until after they began to be translated into Greek
(in the third century BC). In fact, it was well into the
second century AD before most of these books were
given their titles, let alone their chapters and verses.

6

Help From Archaeology

Artist's impression based on archaeological remains of a
family in Jericho around 1600BC

To position our Biblical Books in terms of 'time',
archaeology gives us some valuable dates and
markers:

● **OLD STONE AGE (PALAEOLITHIC) 2-1 MILLION BC.** Who will
complain about the suggestion that our planet Earth is
five billion years old? We know for a fact that plant
and animal life originated here some 500 million
years ago. Some think that 'man' has been living here
now for 1.3 million years – if the recent discovery of
ancient human remains in South Africa is to be

accepted. Apparently, our oldest fossils date from about 600,000 years ago. Neanderthals are said to have evolved some 300,000 years ago and recent anthropological evidence seems to show that, by then, the faculty of speech was operating – though perhaps only haltingly. But much of man's early story is still largely a matter of guesswork.

● 200,000 BC is the date suggested for developing from Homo Erectus. Homo Sapiens and Neanderthals seem to have co-existed. Both are now credited with speech and they will both have contributed in some way to the development of human thinking, and language, of course, would continue to develop along its own evolutionary lines.

● There is little archaeological evidence to suggest human existence as we understand it, much before about 40,000 years ago, of any sort of human settlement apart from cave-dwellings. These provide evidence of advanced design in stone, wood and bone artefacts. Copper and other metal goods begin to appear. Many instances of human migration can be traced – for example, the migration of the Mongols through the Bering Straits into America has been dated to about 20,000 BC – i.e. before the glacial formation of the Rocky Mountain range about 6,000 BC.

● The area with which this Guide is concerned, however, is the 'Near East' – beginning from about 20,000 BC. Here we find the emergence of more permanent settlements that have the following time-scales and characteristics:

● **MIDDLE STONE AGE (MESOLITHIC) 10,000-7,000 BC**. The Human Species now sees the first really basic change in its way of life. From being a nomadic hunter in the previous era, Man develops a life of intensified 'food gathering' – planting crops and domesticating animals. There are some tribal peoples, living in the twentieth century AD that have not as yet developed beyond this stage.

● **NEW STONE AGE (NEOLITHIC) 7,000-4,000 BC.** By now Man had become a fully-fledged food-producer, and was living a more sedentary life. Villages are becoming common and, with them, 'customs' and 'rules'. Remains of such sites (dating from the seventh-millennium BC) have been found, for instance, at Jericho at the southern end of the Dead Sea, showing quite 'advanced' colourfully-decorated pottery. Remains of late fifth-millennium village sites have been found in Egypt and in Western Asia.

● **COPPER-STONE AGE (CHALCOLITHIC) 4,000-3,200 BC.** Farming villages appear, showing an increased specialization in crafts, copper-work, jewellery, and painted pottery etc. Upper Mesopotamia now becomes quite densely settled. Such farming villages become fairly numerous in Palestine. Though China, Middle and South America already had similar developments, apart from Egypt, Lower Mesopotamia shows us the first example of 'civilization' in the Near East, with, in particular, the Sumerian people that occupy the alluvial lands of the lower Tigris and Euphrates rivers. By the end of this period, Egypt had developed 'cooperatives' enabling it to establish two sizeable kingdoms in Upper and Lower Egypt. The Egyptian hieroglyph was already in use when the Sumerians invented writing (cuneiform). [The 'civilized' Incas, interestingly enough, who lived in the period, did not write.]

● EARLY BRONZE AGE 3,200-2050 BC. Leaving pre-history, we arrive at a period that is documented by numerous contemporary inscriptions. As yet there are no 'standard terms' for dating subsequent 'Ages'. The Early Bronze Age is the age of the Pyramids, though the Sphinx is thought to be much older. Egypt is now unified under a Pharaoh, who eventually takes on the status of a god. In total charge and control of his kingdom, he had no cause to provide a 'law code' – in fact, all bureaucracy was administered by a Vizier.

By the middle of the third millennium the development of 'sedentary occupation' reached the southern end of Transjordan, where a Semitic people, the Canaanites, had lived since before the fourth millennium. However, no material culture comparable with that of Mesopotamia or Egypt developed in this area, nor yet, had it established any political unity.

● MIDDLE BRONZE AGE 2050-1550 BC. 'Hurrians', a people originating in what is now Armenia, migrated west and south, and formed a kingdom (Mittani) which eventually reduced Assyria to a petty State. It was these Hurrians who transmitted the Sumero-Akkadian culture. Tablets from the fifteenth and fourteenth centuries BC give valuable insights into the social customs of early Biblical times. By 2,000 BC, another important people of this time, and part of the migration from the north and east, the Hittites (p.30), had infiltrated Asia Minor. [Hittites had sacked Babylon about 1,530 BC – but this 'one-off' attack was to affect that area for another four hundred years.]

THE PATRIARCHS & CONQUEST OF CANAAN

As the nineteenth century BC began, Palestine, was recovering from the effects of Amorite invasions from the north. It was just one such an invasion that included Abraham and his family among its numbers. As settlers, they would have assimilated the language of Canaan and would develop the Canaanite 'city-state' system for the next 500 years, that is, until the Habiru (see p.30) migrations from the south, attempted to destroy the inhabitants.

This period saw the climax in the art of Palestinian ceramics. It was also during the time of 'conquest' that the Habiru people began to form itself into a nation, and, with its first great meeting at Sichem, began to assess itself in terms of its 'history'. Their writings would eventually trace Hebrew development from way back, to what is called the Patriarchal Period, with Abraham, Isaac and Jacob, which starts about 1,850 BC.

While these Patriarchs appear to have been associated with the tail-end of the Amorite migrations, their story is of a later Hebrew construction, which is coloured by the traditions of other peoples living in the surrounding areas. It is important to remember that, while oral traditions continue to develop, it will be nearly 900 years before any of the Hebrews set about writing it down. We will also try to keep in mind that it is their developing ideas, symbolism and language, which will be the means by which they will transmit these happenings.

7

Origins of the 'Tribes' of Israel

Semitic nomads and donkey, suggesting clothing worn by Abraham's family. Taken from tomb of second millennium BC Egyptian nobleman

Consistently poor harvests, due to changing climatic conditions in the north-east of the Mediterranean, resulted in the migration of Hittite and other peoples to Egypt, which they came to control from 1720-1570 BC. Canaanite people would naturally join this migration, as did others from further east. As pioneers, such migrations would have left many behind. Similarly, those who left Egypt with Moses, some 400 years later, would leave behind those who wanted to stay.

We actually know very little of what happened to these migrants in Egypt during the 'four hundred years' between the end of Genesis and the beginning of Exodus, nor do we know how they integrated with Egyptian culture. That they should have maintained their racial identities, throughout their sojourn as 'Habiru' in Egypt, is as unlikely as that they maintained any tribal identity, if by then, they had such identities.

The 'Tribes of Israel' (*aka* Jacob) are said to have left Egypt, with Moses at the head of the column. But none is mentioned by name. Tribal names only start appearing when the settled areas are being marked out. Please remember that the writers of Exodus and Genesis were completing their work about 600 BC onwards. They were merely using earlier traditions to explain, as best they could, the demarcation of these tribal areas, and, at the same time, give their readers sufficient reason for maintaining a situation, which had been their heritage since the time of King David (1000-962 BC).

□

We have evidence of at least two departures – in one, Habiru were 'expelled', and in the other they 'made their escape'. Seeing how migrations happen, there is no reason to suppose these were isolated events. While these could be records of the same event but seen from different points of view, there are good reasons for suggesting that Habiru took different routes, presumably under different leaders. However, in later Hebrew thinking, it was the departure under Moses that became the most

Sheep by the Sea of Galilee

significant event and it was called the 'EXODUS' (the Greek word for 'Exit').[3]

Those pioneers returned to Palestine, where they met up with the descendants of those who had remained 400 years earlier. Inevitably this would cause friction, as it meant the reintegration of those with Egyptian backgrounds with people who, by then, had become totally 'Canaanite' in their customs and mind-set. There was a great meeting at Sichem (today's Nablus, near Samaria) at which the incoming Habiru groups accommodated with some of the indigenous people and arranged the division of their respective areas. These areas were to be named after the 'Hebrew tribes'.

THE ARRIVAL OF SAUL, DAVID AND SOLOMON

Having settled down, the Habiru groups then wanted to be like their neighbours, and have their own kings. First came Saul, then David, then Solomon. It was David who managed to unify this sprawling group into a 'kingdom', but this only lasted a hundred years (c1020 – 922 BC). Such ethnically disparate Habiru groups were unable to maintain this unity much beyond the death of David, and soon broke up. Ten of them formed a 'kingdom' to the north centred on 'Samaria', leaving the southern kingdom of groups centred on 'Jerusalem'. These kingdoms came to be known as 'Israel' and 'Judah' respectively.

3. The Bible Story of the Exodus can be dated during the nineteenth Egyptian dynasty (about 1300 BC).

The tribal stability, vital to David's idea of 'Hebrew' unity, was now lost. Intermittent strife between Israel and Judah then followed, laying both open to eventual destruction by their powerful neighbours. It was during the period that followed these events that the actual Biblical writing began. It was a work that was to take a good 500 years to complete.

□

We looked briefly at Hittite migrations, which were a continuing phenomenon. Within another 500 years, as they retraced their steps, many so-called Habiru settled in Canaan. Ethnic resemblances will have resulted in groupings, which were designated as 'Tribes'. During the composition of Exodus, the tribes needed to be associated with the Patriarchs, and so were given names, which corresponded with one of the twelve sons of Jacob, (aka Israel), the last of the Patriarchs.

Apart from the others, Jacob had two sons by Rachel – Joseph and Benjamin. (One pre-Exodus tradition has Rachel giving seven sons to Jacob; yet another says she gave him fourteen.) The names of twelve brothers are listed (Gen.46:8-27) with their own offspring, but, otherwise, few are ever named individually.

JOSEPH'S SONS

Most have heard of Joseph and his 'technicolour dream coat'. His is the longest story in the Old Testament (Gen.37-50), yet no tribe is named after

Joseph. Instead, we have the tribes of 'Ephraim' and 'Manasseh', Joseph's sons.

Reuben is the eldest of Jacob's family and its spokesman. Judah is also a spokesman. It is *his* name that is later given to the southern kingdom, the land of Judah, and, by the time of Christ, his is the last 'recognizable' tribe to have survived.

The Term 'Jew' Arrives

The Jewish people were designated 'Jews' in the sixth century BC because 'Judah', a twenty-five-square-mile area, was all that was left of their country.

☐

Once they had settled in Canaan, under the leadership of Joshua and others, names were given to particular tribal areas which would coincide with the traditional names of Jacob's sons – if only to keep in the popular mind, the Promise that God had made to their ancestors. In this, the tribal names are vital since they serve as a link back to the Patriarchs. Both the Books of Exodus and Numbers begin with a list of the Tribes. Numbers (Chapters 13, 25 and 34) repeats the list with some changes.

They called a meeting at Sichem to consolidate these tribal areas, and, in order to demonstrate their new position and, to compare favourably with their neighbours, they produced their own kings. Though there was initial hostility to the monarchy, the kingdom was united under David, but disintegrated after only a hundred years as the surrounding peoples, Philistines and the Arameans regained power and independence.

The secession of some Hebrew tribes resulted in the creation of a separate 'Northern Kingdom' with its capital at Samaria. The '**D**' Tradition (see p.83) relates this story in the 1st and 2nd Books of Kings. The Book of Amos (7:13 and 8:14) adds that the setting up of 'rival' temples merely consolidated the division.

Even though, for a time, Israel treated Judah as little more than a vassal state, (agreeing to help out when either was engaged with recalcitrant tribes) the North unwittingly made injudicious agreements with its neighbours, which made her vulnerable. The significance of the northern king 'not being of David's line' was soon realized. Weak leadership on the part of its kings was exploited by their priests and seers who tried in vain to prevent their 'kings' making concordats with Assyria, which ultimately led to the Fall of Samaria in 721 BC.

It was also the injudicious foreign policies of the South, which later resulted in the Fall of Jerusalem in 583 BC. First the Northern Kingdom was destroyed and the Hebrews there enslaved; then, two hundred years later, the same fate befell the Southern Kingdom – this time at the hands of the Babylonians. It is a pity that the Bible dismisses the northern King Omri (876-869 BC) with a few citations, since he was the peace-maker who was highly praised by the Assyrian, Sargon II.

Those fateful events, the total loss of their king-doms, did great damage to Hebrew self-awareness and self-confidence. The religious preaching and writing from this particular time, was a mixture of advice and recrimination. The 'I told you God would punish us like this, if we disobeyed His Law' was coupled with the 'Remember that our lot is to be "Habiru", an exiled, "foreign" people, which is why we were thrown out of Egypt. It is not God's fault.' It was a combination of 'What more can we expect for our unfaithfulness?' and 'God is faithful to his promises – so all will be well.'

Summary of the Habiru History

We know now why Egypt was full of Habiru. Some of those who migrated northwards, settled in Canaan and eventually came to write their story. When they did, it was surprisingly like everyone else's story as is seen in the way they accounted for what happened *before* their experiences in Egypt. We see this in their accounts of their Patriarchs – Abraham, Isaac and Jacob (pp.28 & 35) ending up with Jacob's son, Joseph.

While these stories of the Patriarchs were compiled later, the Habiru's own particular 'history' begins with the Book of Exodus, which tells of their escape from their 'enslavement' in Egypt. With hindsight operating, they describe their escape as being arranged by their God under the leadership of Moses, whose mission it was to take them back home, to the land promised to them in a Pact made by God (Genesis 12).

During this journey, which is also traced in the Book of Numbers Ch.33, God makes a fresh Pact with His people, which now stipulates some conditions: 'Be completely and exclusively loyal to Me by keeping my Law and all will be well with you. Trusting in Me means that you will make no pacts with other peoples. Oh!, and don't forget, worship no other gods but Me!' (Exodus 19 and 20).

The terms of this Pact, or Covenant, are well summarized in the Ten Commandments. But the misery and impatience of the people grew as they journeyed away from Egypt, culminating in a general refusal to believe in the Pact.[4] After this rebellion had been resolved, the people crossed the Jordan under Moses' successor, Joshua. His followers, then led by the Judges, continued their conquest of the indigenous Canaanites, and eventually settled and divided their land according to their settlements.

They then pleaded for a King, which was arranged by one, Samuel, who first of all crowned Saul for them. David, his successor, united the groups. Simply put, these groups took the names of the 'Twelve Tribes of Israel'. The Genesis saga then appears to have been used to account for *their* origins.

THE SAMARITANS

David's unified kingdom could not survive ethnic inter-tribal rivalry. The resulting rift divided the people – North and South. Under inept leadership, what came to be called the Northern Kingdom, departed from the Pact that God had renewed with the Hebrews while they were still a united people and began to adopt the idolatrous practices of their successful Assyrian neighbours.

The prophets, Elijah, Amos and Hosea took over the leadership but, lacking David's kingly charisma, they could not persuade them to return to this Pact. While they may have understood that Yahweh was in total command, we are told that Yahweh then

4. Such rebellions are detailed in the Book of Numbers 11:1-15, 14:1-4, 27-35, 16:13-15, 20:2-5, 21:5.

allowed their erstwhile friends, the Assyrians, to discipline them. This meant the destruction of their capital, Samaria (721BC) and the execution or imprisonment of their leaders.

The Assyrians then brought in their own people with whom the surviving Hebrews integrated, thus further diminishing their idea of the importance of the Pact. No longer to be trusted by their southern compatriots, the Northern Hebrews were seen as an heretical, schismatic sect. Due to this breach, the Northerners became known as 'Samaritans'. The prophet Ezra managed to reimpose the Law of God in the Southern Kingdom – and also on the Samaritans. But though the Northern Hebrews kept it up to a point, they then further alienated themselves from the loyal Hebrew people to the South by building their own temple.

From its privileged position centred on David's city, Jerusalem, the Southern Kingdom, may have felt that the North had got its just deserts. Generally speaking though, the South was fortunate to have good and religious kings. But their real guarantee of a secure future was the continued existence of Solomon's Temple.

However, instead of learning from the fate of their northern compatriots and reinforcing their God-given Pact, these southerners began to slacken their traditional religious practices. Despite the encourage-ment of prophets like Isaiah, Micah and Jeremiah, who warned them of what would happen if they did not cease their idolatrous practices (always a great temptation), within 200 years they were to suffer the same fate as the Northern Kingdom. This time they were reduced by the Babylonians. Destroying Jerusalem including Solomon's magnificent Temple, the Babylonians executed, or imprisoned, all who might incite revenge.

SUMMARY

Starting with King Saul, this epic yarn is found in the Books of Samuel and Kings. A different version of these events is given in The Book of Chronicles. By now, of course, as the writing begins, the Hebrews begin to describe themselves as 'a disappointment to God' and, in the destruction of Jerusalem, recognize His punishment for their unfaithfulness. This idea of 'suffering' as the price of 'infidelity to the Pact', was to colour not only all Hebrew writings, but also, later, the thinking of Christendom.

It was an idea that was actually introduced in the Book of Genesis, where the reason given for the existence of 'suffering' was Adam's original act of disobedience.[5] The prophets, Ezekiel and Jeremiah, would proclaim later that God really does love his people and is still in control. Yet the Bible shows God's hand in the eventual collapse of the Babylonians at the hands of the Persians, whose leader Cyrus II (described by Isaiah as a 'messiah') arranges for the Hebrew exiles in Babylon to be sent home.

The story of the resettlement of the Hebrews in Judah, from 538 BC, is told by two friends Nehemiah

---

5. The traditional understanding of Adam's punishment is his expulsion from the Garden of Eden. Genesis 3:23 however, gives quite a different explanation as is seen on page 92.

and Ezra; while their religious development was directed by the prophets Haggai, Zechariah – and lastly by Malachi, who marks the end of the time of the Prophets.

8

The Written Word Begins to Appear

Reconstruction of a fortress city at Megiddo, presumed to have been built by Solomon around 1000BC. Architectural remains have enabled scholars to build a scale model

Standing in the magnificent city of Jerusalem in 800BC and looking back into the past, it would have been crystal clear, that, whatever had happened in the interim, it was in their Escape from Egypt some 400 years before, that the nation of Hebrews began to realize itself as 'a People'. The way the Exodus is written gives the story of a momentous rescue. Since

Third-century BC Sidonian burial cave at Tel Maresha, Israel

such a rescue was beyond their ability as slaves to organize, it must have been arranged by one of the gods. The big question for the Habiru, then, was to find which god had been responsible.

By the time the definitive account of the Exodus was produced (between 500-400BC), they had settled for one God. Their search for a 'one-God' scenario is shown in the different names they used. All their names for God were pagan because those were the only divine names available.

To complicate matters, the separation of the two kingdoms, Israel from Judah, brought with it a divergence of ideas. Though these two separate Hebrew groups, North and South, clearly shared the same background and traditions, by the time they began to compose their writings they had developed different ways of speaking about their common history. As the two groups drifted apart the influence of the oracles and prophets in the North produced a fresh way of looking at the past. It was not until the significance of the separation of these two Kingdoms became apparent, that their different approach to their history, and the reasons for the distinctive differences in their Biblical writing, would even be appreciated – let alone be understood. We will see this when we examine the Traditions used by those who wrote the Bible. (p.77ff).

When was the Pentateuch Written?

Scholarship now confirms that all the books of the Bible were written long after the events that are recorded; we also know that those events were carefully selected to indicate the significance of the final outcome. This is especially true of the New Testament, when it had become clear that the Messiah had at last been recognized for who He really was. But like much other literature, the Bible once it has been read through, readers are left, looking expectantly for the next instalment!

We can be fairly certain that the first five Books of the Bible were still being constructed as late as 400 BC, even though some of them had been started over 600 years before. For the Hebrews, the Exodus is the beginning of their history as a people. Eventually they would need to explain for themselves how they came to be in Egypt; and then to explain how they came to understand that their homeland was to be along the 'West Bank of the Jordan' as it is now called.

LATER HISTORICAL DEVELOPMENTS

By 530 BC Hebrew territory had shrunk considerably since Joshua's time. Persia was now its most powerful neighbour; that is until the Greek rulers in Egypt (the Ptolemies) in their struggle for power against the Syrian/Persian Kings (Seleucids), took over in the fourth and third centuries BC.

Translating the Hebrew Scriptures for the growing numbers of Greek-speaking Jews in Alexandria may have been a regrettable necessity, but, then, it was part of the Hellenist attempt to swamp the Middle East with the new Greek culture. To the Jews in Palestine, Hellenism was an anathema. Having at long last been successfully weaned from ritual paganism, their little country, Judah, now revolted against any alien attempt to corrupt its traditions. The famous Maccabean revolt of 168 BC saw many Jews preferring to die rather than change their exclusive way of life. Happily, this revolt not only succeeded in enlarging Jewish territory – it also obtained for them some religious and political freedom. Their country now stretched the length of the West Bank and, with Galilee, also included Samaria.

ARRIVAL OF THE MESSIAH

It was now ruled by a number of High Priests (Hasmoneans) who managed to effect an amicable relationship with the next great power in the Near East, the Romans, who then annexed the whole area to form part of its Persian protectorate (63 BC). It was while the Romans were strengthening the Middle Eastern trade routes, that the Messiah, promised to the Hebrews centuries before, was born.

A combination of Hebrew and Greek provided the Messiah with the holy name 'Jesus Christ'. This Messiah made a notable impact on the people, providing a fresh understanding to the Hebrew traditions which were already familiar to everyone. Like all teachers before him, he chose disciples. But accounts of his words and actions brought him to the attention of the aristocratic Pharisee families. They considered him a threat not only to good order but also to traditional religious discipline, for which they had made themselves responsible.

Strangely enough, not only were the Pharisees

unaware of the tribe to which Jesus belonged, but knew nothing of his family or background. It seems, from the Gospel accounts, that without making any enquiries, they concluded that the popular notion that he might be the promised Messiah was probably left-wing hype. To preclude prolonged agitation they had him executed. Whereas those who would listen, the Messiah proclaimed the Coming of God's King-dom, the Forgiveness of Man's Sin and the destruc-tion of Death, the seeds of which were all to be found in Hebrew expectations.

THE CHRIST AND THE 'GREAT CONTINUUM'

While this description follows 'later historical developments' we need to remind ourselves that the Bible is not a chronological work of 'history'. We can attempt to place it in an historical setting, but it is, from start to finish, a 'theological work'.

Of course it is an interesting exercise to try to fit its composition into a secular historical framework, but none of its contributors had any sense of following, or including, secular developments. From the time of Ezra, not only would they have nothing to do with what was going on around them, but would fight to protect themselves from all outside influences. This was the 'theological approach' preached by the Messiah and his disciples.

The Christ's appearance, alive among his friends, after he been buried, was at first unbelievable. But once accepted as fact, it became the main feature of the second part of the Bible called the New Testament. The accounts in the New Testament show that everything previously belonging to Hebrew religious heritage was strictly adhered to and largely kept intact. But its meaning was to change almost beyond recognition. This would involve certain adjustments to traditional Jewish observances that would be made gradually. The words of the Hebrew Bible would remain unchanged but, for the followers of this Messiah figure, they were to look and sound quite different.

The compilers of the New Testament saw such developments as being the work of the Holy Spirit. The active presence of the Holy Spirit was as recognizable to the Hebrews at the end of the Biblical period as it had been in the Creation narrative in Genesis, and as it had been throughout their history. For the contributors to the New Testament it was the same Holy Spirit who arranged the Birth of the Christ, His Resurrection and His Ascension, as had been present at the Creation. But, as this was *New* Testament material, the traditional Jewish mind would not accept it.

The New Testament appears to chart another 'Beginning', where a *new* Covenant is mentioned; yet another view shows that, far from being a 'Beginning', it is merely a further theological development, part of the 'Great Continuum'. This development was to 'extend' Man beyond the 'Cosmos' of Biblical times, which began with the choice of a People, through the Christ phenomenon, and on into the future. . .until – who knows – the end of Time, and, perhaps, even beyond that.

David and Alexander: An Interesting Parallel

DAVID was to the Hebrews what Alexander the Great was to the Greeks – and though 700 years separate them, the similarities are noteworthy. Both started their careers when scarcely teenagers. The leadership qualities of both were readily recognized; as soldiers, they were highly successful in military strategy. While both had close friends, they also made implacable enemies. Both had a special relationship with the gods and both led charmed lives. David is told he is 'son of god' by the prophet Nathan (2Sam.7:14 and Psalm 2:7); Alexander is told he is 'son of god' by the Oracle at Siva. Poems and songs celebrating these two heroes, are unique for their vintage and are repeated with enthusiasm to this day.

SUMMARY

As a Guide to an idea of how the Bible originated, we have moved through some 200,000 years of development. From the time of primitive hunters, we have seen civilized peoples living in communities, some of whom were peace-loving – some not. They all show developed and sophisticated origins, which explained their behaviour; they all survive in atmospheres of continually improving relations – but, sadly for some, the weakest disintegrate.

So far, the Bible traces only the cultural development of the *Hebrews*. This culture, which they had described in theological terms, was to undergo a colossal rejuvenation once it had grown into what is now called 'Christendom'.

View of Mount Sinai

9

Exploring the Structure of the Bible

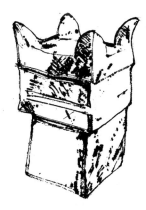

Tenth century BC limestone altar from Megiddo, exactly like
the one described in the Book of Kings

Like searching among the foundations of the castle,
we are going to look at four distinct areas of the
foundations. These are the Traditions, the existence of
which, until recently, had never even been imagined.
The Biblical foundations are found first in the 'Traditions' and the use these make of the 'Materials'.

In a criminal case, the charge is read and
evidence, covering the available facts, is provided

by different witnesses (each with a different point of view). Counsels for both Prosecution and Defence, with access to all the evidence, use it to promote their particular view of the facts, for or against a guilty verdict. The Jury then decides on the matter according to Law.

The 'four distinct Traditions' in the Bible follow similar narratives but, their different points of view show that they use the materials at their disposal very differently. Since most witnesses in any enquiry are unlikely to be 'professional observers', no one is surprised to find the odd mistaken observation.

Within the First Five Books of the Bible we find evidence coming from different times and from different places hence these different Traditions. They have been stitched together, as it were, by a group of people called 'redactors' who have produced a theological narrative.

A redactor (a special sort of 'editor') is one, or more people, who, at different times, have arranged and rearranged these traditions, in order to build such a story. But this has also been done in such a way so as not to lose anything that might enhance the overall picture. Thus, we find that, in the process, the 'story-line' often gets repeated.

These different Traditions are clearly recognizable. Not only have they a tendency to favour a different name for 'God' but also that their stories are constructed differently as they clearly use different expressions. It is these that appear to be the principal Traditions (foundations) used by the redactor; but besides these, there were still other sources. These other sources, especially the orally transmitted meditations on the 'facts', give scholars a lot of fun, principally because, while their presence can still be detected, their origins are extremely elusive. The original 'documents' of course, no longer exist. All that we have to go on now are the copies.

THE FOUR 'TRADITIONS' IN THE AUTHORSHIP OF THE BIBLE: AN EXERCISE IN DETECTION

(1) THE 'J' ('YAHWIST') TRADITION

The 'Yahwist' **'J'** Tradition clearly favoured the name 'Jehovah' ('Yahovah')[6] as this is the only name for God that is used. (Compare the different ways 'God' is mentioned in Genesis, Chapters 1, 2 and 3). **'J'** appears to be the first or earliest writer to show how Israel's distinguished 'history' compares favourably with that of Egypt and Mesopotamia. **'J'** is also the first to show that the Hebrews were aware of God entering human history 'in time'. This was unique in contemporary literature.

The **'J'** tradition first appears during the time of Solomon (who had close ties with Egypt) and continues throughout the duration of the Southern Kingdom (Judah). David is seen, not only as 'god's

---

6. 'Jahovah' is the German form, hence 'J'. When the sacred name 'Yahweh' ceased to be pronounced (for reasons of sacred correctness), 'Adonai' took its place (see the Hebrew Masoretic Text). The pagan god, 'Yah' or 'Ya'u', a name probably known to Abraham, is suggested as the original form of Yahweh. Moses' father-in-law was a priest of Yahu, the Moon god.

son' but also God's 'representative'. In **'J'**, David provides the political and religious thrust to this developing nation, and at the same time reflects the ongoing promise that God made to his ancestors.

In **'J'**, David does not appear as the absolute monarch of the type found in other countries, but is portrayed as the King who acts in the service of his god and of his people (an Egyptian notion).

'J' is the Tradition that changes the name 'Habiru' (later changed to 'Hebrews'), to 'Israel'. (What can be confusing is to find the name 'Israel' being used by other traditions to designate the *Northern* Kingdom) From about 538 BC the Persians decided that those Hebrew people who were repatriated, to the then smaller area called Judea, should be called 'Jews'.

However, **'J'** may not be, chronologically, the first of the four Traditions, because it uses material from the other traditions that are to be found in the Biblical Books, (e.g. 2 Samuel and 1 Kings). Even so, we can be certain now that the **'J'** Tradition was the first to be used in the composition of the Hebrew Creation story – but not the last! We can also tell that it was composed to explain Israel to Israel, and was therefore not intended for Gentiles (who were 'non-Jews' and who would have no experience of Hebrew traditions).

The writer(s) of the **'J'** Tradition also believed that Israel's 'Habiru-ancestors' were in fact the origin of all Mankind! The **'J'** Tradition, with its concept of 'Man-related-to-his-world', actually has no parallel in any other Near Eastern folklore of the first millennium BC.

'**J**' is also the genius responsible for that unique idea of 'Election' in which the Hebrew God 'freely chose a race of people' as his own, even though it possessed no notable qualities to recommend it. Then, as all 'Myths' tend to do, '**J**' projects this idea backwards, to the beginning of things, so that 'God's choice' gets reflected in the story of Cain and Abel, Noah & Co., and, of course, in the story of Abraham and his descendants.

Finally, '**J**' is preoccupied with the preservation of the 'family line' and is chiefly responsible for those stories that detail what God does to ensure that, like with Noah and Jacob, David's line is preserved.

(2) THE 'E' ('ELOHIST') TRADITION

The 'Elohist' '**E**' Tradition. Though ten of the twelve tribes separated and consolidated themselves in the North, the Hebrews remained one nation with one background history. The North set up its own king – because all groups, making a fresh start, did that. But their king was not of David's family (not the 'Lord's anointed'), and so could not possibly be their leader in the same sense that David was. But the North accepted the Prophets, to whom it fell to encourage the people to keep the Law.

While the '**J**' Tradition began in the South, the '**E**' tradition began in the North and, though the overall story follows the same theme of that composed in the South, the whole tone and context is different. The Northern approach is not about 'kings' or even leadership; but about maintaining God's supremacy. The prophets show this in preferring to promote 'loyal

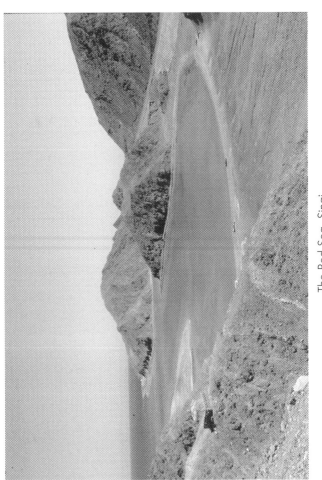

The Red Sea, Sinai

moral behaviour', rather than encouraging the people to follow a kingly leader in the manner of companies of soldiers under military command.

Both the **'E'** and **'J'** Traditions speak of Abraham. Sometimes one can see how these two traditions interweave, where for example, one moment Abraham is described as a shepherd (North) and then next he appears to be a commanding general (South).

Both **'E'** and **'J'** Traditions seem to have accepted that the Hebrews have already integrated with contemporary pagan traditions, so that one can see the **'E'** Tradition following the development of the 'pagan thread' as it grew into the 'one-God' religion of Israel. We are almost certain now that the Habiru's ancestral god, 'El', became fused with the Canaanite 'El'.

The evidence for this dates from about 1500BC. Contemporary pagans called their chief god: 'El', El'yon, El'shaddai, El'ohim, Ya' (hence -Yahweh) (cf Ps.91), El' Berith, El' Roi, Olam etc. 'Baal', however, was one of the Canaanite gods (as was Enlil, Dagon, Nergal and Anu etc.). Canaanite myth has 'Baal' replacing 'El' when he 'retires' as head of the 'divine group', the 'Elim'.

The **'E'** Tradition, in some places, merely parallels earlier **'J'** stories. We still do not know why it was not copied out in full, like some other parallel stories, but seems only to have been used as a supplement to **'J'**. While **'J'** is a Southern construction, the **'E'** Tradition not only reflects the prophetic tradition of the Northern Kingdom, but also adds details that heighten the suspense of some of the **'J'** stories. (Some of the Psalms are entirely from the **'E'** Tradition.)

(3) THE 'P' ('PRIESTLY') TRADITION

The 'Priestly' **'P'** Tradition was probably composed during the latter part of the sixth century BC. It reflects the 'Priestly' concerns which appear in the lengthy legal sections found throughout the Pentateuch. Apart from his contribution to the Stories of the Creation and the Flood, **'P'** hardly appears in Genesis except to bring some order into it. Without **'P'** giving it some cohesion, Genesis would have been a haphazard arrangement of the materials provided by the **'J'** and **'E'** Traditions.

The **'P'** Tradition seems to have been introduced during and after the Exile – i.e., late sixth century BC – as the Temple is rebuilt. Its 'priestly interests' are seen in the careful way all Israel's ancient religious rites are codified and up-dated. They are then brought into the Liturgy of the Temple after it had been restored (538BC). [You find this in the Book of Ezra.] These ancient rites had a special place in the Liturgy and Ezra shows this ritual as having been intended by God for Israel, from the very beginning. You would, therefore, expect it to be reflected in **'P'**'s contribution to the Creation and Flood stories, which actually appears in verses of praise and thanksgiving. [**'P'** is probably responsible for the first mention of 'sacrifice' in the Bible, in the story of Cain and Abel (Genesis: Chapter 4).]

The destruction of Jerusalem and the Exile by the Babylonians (580BC) gave the Hebrews two serious problems. The first was 'the loss of their promised homeland' and the second was 'the unjustified contempt heaped on them by their persecutors'. Both are vividly presented in the **'P'** Tradition – quite unlike the **'J'** and **'E'** Traditions, which prefer to use 'myth' to connect Israel with its past.

By avoiding 'myth', **'P'** tended to overshadow both **'J'** and **'E'** in importance, since, by the time **'P'** appeared, 'myth' was thought to smack too much of 'paganism'. This is another reason for suggesting the redactor's preference for the **'P'** Tradition to provide his readers with the first words of the Hebrew Creation Story. Though **'J'** is actually responsible for the Genesis story of Man's expulsion from the Garden of Eden, it may well be, that, because of that story's 'myth' content, **'P'** makes no mention of it!

(4) THE 'D' ('HISTORICAL') TRADITION

The 'Historical' **'D'** Tradition is a rather later discovery. It has been detected in those parts of the Pentateuch that cannot be readily attributed to the **'J'**, **'E'** or **'P'** Traditions. **'D'** is the 'historian' who is interested in 'chronology' and has his own way of 'dating' events. This is clear in the Book of Deuteronomy Chapter 5:1, which has a separate account of the Moses' experience on a mountain. While most people claim that Moses met his God on 'Mount Sinai' – **'D'** has Moses on 'Mount Horeb'. This may be another name for the same place, but it could also be somewhere else.

This does not mean that there were two different occasions when Moses is reported to have received the Ten Commandments; it is just another account of the same event but from a different angle. But we find at least one Tradition that shows Moses and his company taking a different route as they travelled home. 'X marking the spot' may well be a quite recent study, but trying to locate ancient sites merely from references in the Bible and other contemporary traditions is at least questionable if not impossible.

For another example you might compare the story of the Ten Commandments in the Book of Deuteronomy 5:1-22 with the same story told in Exodus 20:1-21. Among many examples of this sort of thing, we find Matthew's Gospel making a point of Christ's Sermon being 'on the Mount', whereas Luke places it firmly 'on the Plain'.

It is the genius of the redactor, as 'the weaving compiler' of the Books in the Old Testament, that has put all these Traditions together; but as yet no one has ever thought of him as the author of the Pentateuch.

SUMMARY

The **'J'** Tradition relates the Hebrew understandings as they are found in the Southern Kingdom.
The **'E'** Tradition relates the Hebrew understandings as they are found in the Northern Kingdom.
The **'P'** Tradition traces the development of the Hebrew Law.
The **'D'** Tradition was found in the Temple and gives the Bible the closest approach to ancient Hebrew history.

$$\boxed{10}$$

Exploring Genesis

Bas-relief showing procession of Judean exiles departing Lachish after its subjugation be Assyrian aggressors (under Sennacherib) in 701BC

HISTORICAL BACKGROUND

Though indigenous Canaanites were writing from c1370BC, being late developers, few Habiru knew 'writing'. We ought not to assume that Genesis is the work of one writer, but rather several contributors, working at different speeds, with different agendas, in different places, and probably independently. But once the writing begins, as we have seen, we get to recognize the existence of these separate 'Traditions'.

Besides the Traditions, the Habiru also worked on what we call their 'Materials'. For example, they used oral traditions (those handed down from memory), so it is unlikely that the writers were also responsible for the oral tradition. It is for such reasons as these that the first five Books of the Bible took over 600 years to complete, and why we can now at last discard the ancient notion that Moses alone was responsible for the Pentateuch.

The 'Materials' used in Genesis include the raw pieces of 'myth', 'genealogies' and 'legend' that identifies the mindset common to the ancient cultures of the Near East. Written in forms that would strike chords in the Hebrew mind, they have lain there undetected until recently. Though many have been recovered, it is ages since such primitive memorabilia ceased to be included in any living literature. But 'myth' is found in all ancient literatures, which tell creation stories that show Man being fixed in his place through the power of a mixture of 'gods' and 'cosmic forces'.

The Priestly Tradition 'P' emerges as Israel's 'temple religion' is developing well. By now 'Myth' is out! But 'P' reluctantly uses 'Myth', in the absence of any other explanation, to demonstrate his unique idea: 'first, one God and, after the rest of Creation, one man' as in Genesis Chapter 1.

Genesis actually contains more than two Creation stories, but none of them is 'mythical' in the same way. With all their differences, 'P's thread of ritual can be seen, both in the repetition of these stories and in their 're-enactment'. We need to remember that 'ritual' was essential to mythology. But 'P' escapes from the 'mythology' trap by making these stories look like 'prose poems'. He writes them to celebrate the dominant Israelite dogmatic convictions regarding the nature of God's Creation and its consequences – as he understood them – between 800-600BC.

Genesis 6:1-4 records a legend that is often found in ancient mythologies, where a peculiar union of gods and humans produced a race of giants. This material comes from the **'J'** Tradition. This legend is used to reflect 'cosmic disorder' in order to show how **'J'** understood Man's growing estrangement from God. Such a unique and profound understanding of Man's shortcomings has effectively darkened his view of the world as it was when *he* was writing – when it was clearly a 'disordered world'. It now becomes easier to see **'J'** being the genius who produced the unique idea of 'Election', in which, 'In his Promise to Abraham, God freely chooses an insignificant race of people' and will lift them out of this 'disordered world'.

The Genealogies of Genesis

The 'Genealogies' that cause headaches to those reading the Bible aloud, are essential in providing the structure in Genesis. They are the products of the **'P'** Tradition. **'P'**, who sees the Habiru (Hebrews) as a 'tribe', is more interested in his cast of players than in dates! [Interestingly – you will not find dates in 'mythology' – they are 'outside time' (p.42)].

These Genealogies continually remind the reader of the 'historical' link between what was happening at the 'time-of-writing', with what was happening in the mists of 'pre-history'. It is the Genealogies in Genesis that distinguish it from the 'never-never' mind-set we find reflected in all other contemporary mythological material.

Of the Materials used in Genesis, 'narrative' provides the largest amount, since Genesis is basically a set of stories linked together. Some stories are repeated, often with differently named 'characters' acting in different circumstances. It is therefore possible that many of them had separate origins. On top of that, all these 'characters' may well have had prior, independent and even different meanings before they got woven into the sources.

IMPORTANCE OF 'MYTH' AND 'LEGEND'

'Legends' are often supported by the myths with which they are then combined. The legends of the Patriarchs (which begin in Gen.12) have preserved, in a primitive sense, the 'history' of 'Things-that-really-Happened', but which is not 'history' in any modern sense. We know we cannot possibly document the creation of Man and his world, or the origin of his dignity, his dependence on God, his successes and failures, as the Bible shows happening in a primordial past. All those stories pre-dated even the vaguest kind of historical memory. From the beginning of this period there was only myth.

However, the genius of the 'J' and 'P' Traditions lies not just their use of 'myth' (Ch.5) to construct an independent story of Man; for them to have done otherwise would have been impossible. Their genius lies in their choice of the best ones while discarding the others.

A myth story, of course, can be 'good', 'indifferent', 'trivial', or 'unspeakably vicious'. Modern research, however, has made it possible to compare ancient mythologies, and confirms what over 3,000 years worth of readers of Genesis have always known, without perhaps realizing it, that each of these four Traditions chose its 'myths' wisely and well.

For 'Epic', the **'J'** and **'P'** Traditions appear to have been combined to produce the Story of the Flood (Gen.6-9). This is clearly a parallel of the story in the great Babylonian *Gilgamesh* myth-cycle. Such a parallel, including so many details, could hardly be a coincidence. Clearly, this 'myth', and the other stories that were put together by the sources of Genesis, have a relatively close common ancestor! Comparing these stories, you find their authors had different agendas, as can be seen in the different ways they used this material.

The Genesis account of the 'Flood', for example, is not part of a 'myth' about a 'divine-cum-human arrangement'. It was just an attempt to explain man's desire for immortality and god-ship, as is seen in the parallel *Gilgamesh* story with its Adam-Noah-like character, Utanapishtim. Instead, the Genesis Flood Story is made into a primitive piece of 'history' that is 'acted out' in a Hollywood 'Warner Brothers'-style epic.

Such a picture reflects a relatively modern approach to reality, portrayed in a 'catastrophic yet natural event' – which also provides the spring-board for what is to happen next! But once you reach the end of the *Gilgamesh* story – that's it – there is nothing to follow!

Most patriarchal 'histories' are best described as 'Sagas'. Saga focuses on the single hero with other characters playing subordinate roles. The stories built around this hero, are tales that might once have referred to, or even belonged to someone else. Saga tales are legends that tell of great and notable characters of the past. (There is a short but clear instance of 'saga' in the Lamech poem in Gen.4: 23-24.)

Closing this section on the Materials used in Genesis, we find that, while 'God created everything', 'everything' does not include building, writing, language, nor does it include man's shortcomings. The absence of adequate information allows the writers of Genesis to account for these by the simple expedient of aetiology – a word for 'the business of finding and assigning appropriate causes for recognized events or happenings'. [For example: Gen.4:17-21 introduces Cain's family merely to account for the origin of some 'arts and crafts': while Gen.10 uses genealogies to show how the tribes, countries and languages originate.]

FROM THE CREATION TO BABEL

On the second page of the Book of Genesis we find the first story of Creation being repeated – but this time back to front. Instead of providing an ordered list of what is created, finishing with the creation of Man, the second account begins with the creation of Man and is less detailed. A serpent then appears and is severely punished for cleverly introducing 'disobedience' as having a beneficial potential!

The Hebrew, and the subsequent thinking of Christendom, believes that 'Adam and Eve were expelled from the Garden of Eden as a punishment

Old water well from the Roman period

for their disobedience'. However, this expulsion, far from being a punishment, is to prevent Eve and her husband (having now become like Yahweh, God), from getting at the fruit that would give them eternal life. (Gen.3:23-24)

Then comes the curious yet famous story of the sacrifice made by Cain and Abel, which ends in bloodshed, whereupon another punishment is meted out. Next, members of Cain's family appear to explain the origins of all the day-to-day necessities of life. Then follows an extensively detailed genealogy.

'Wickedness' is re-introduced as the cause for God's regretting having started the Creation in the first place – a problem which is solved by the Flood. It is Noah's survival that introduces the third account of the Creation story, where we first meet the name 'Canaan' whose native people are much later to become 'slaves of Yahweh'.

Another genealogy is followed by yet another 'regret' story, which ends with the 'scattering' of the people – the story of the Tower of Babel. This is followed by yet another genealogy, which culminates with a man called Terah, the father of Abraham, who decides to join a migration.

This digest covers briefly the preamble or prologue to the Abraham story. It is the Abraham story with which the Hebrews are most interested, since he is the Patriarch who, by tradition, is said to be the original ancestor of this people. [Rather than Adam, Abraham is clearly the more easily recognizable progenitor of the Hebrew Nation.]

The rest of the Book of Genesis extends the Story

of Abraham's descendants and how they eventually end up in Egypt.

By the time you reach the Abraham saga (Gen.11), you will have seen the differences between all the various Creation stories. Modern authors are satisfied to tell their stories as they happen. While some freely use a 'flash-back' technique to highlight certain aspects of their narratives, it is quite unusual for writers to go over the same ground several times. These curious 'repetitions' in the early Books of the Bible give a clue to existence of the Traditions, and why the editors should have felt the need to ensure that they were all included.

THE THREE 'SAGAS' OF GENESIS

There are three main Sagas in Genesis: 1) the Abraham saga; 2) the Jacob (Israel) saga; 3) the Joseph saga. We have to say that these sagas are cult legends associated with ancient southern or central Palestinian religious 'sanctuaries'. Such legends clearly retained great significance since '**J**' has chosen them in his work on Genesis.

But the Joseph saga, like a novelette, has no obvious *religious* aspirations! Unlike his forebears, Joseph shows no prophetic or priestly interests. Joseph does not build altars for sacrifice as the others do, but he is seen as the ideal of the wise Hebrew, who, like Esther, reaches the highest position among his people, short of being king.

We have looked at some of the Materials used in

Genesis. By and large these have been happily assimilated into the Traditions to which they seem to belong. We should not be too concerned about the apparent inconsistencies in the stories, as these did not worry the editors who were the first to choose then from the vast amount and great variety of materials with which to work.

□

Just one example of these inconsistencies is the first and sudden appearance of Cain's 'wife' in a context to which, originally, she did not belong (Gen. 4:17). Another example is that Cain, curiously, presumes the presence of a crowd of 'vengeance-seekers' (Gen. 4:14) but no explanation is given for their presence or where they came from. We may well wonder what business they had in a story that had been adapted to announce Man's First Generation (Gen. 4:1-2). . . and, since they are presumably related to Cain, how is that they are all against him?

The question that is often asked: Since Adam and Eve had two sons, whom did Cain and Abel marry? There are plenty of glib answers on offer, but Genesis is primarily a theological work, and the mythical nature of this section is not concerned with such a thing. Had the *writers* considered this important, they would have given an explanation.

SUMMARY

Dealing with the way Biblical writers used the Traditions and the Materials they had at their disposal will give some idea of how they tackled the then unique idea that there was only one God. When surrounded by cultures that rejoiced in a pantheon of gods, the Hebrews had difficulty in purveying monotheism even amongst themselves. This is why the Prophets had such difficulties in persuading their people to stay clear of multi-god paganism and keep to their 'uniquely' God-given Rules. Roman Europe would not recognize these Rules as such for another 600 years.

11

Exploring The Decalogue

Bedouin with herd of sheep in Sinai peninsular, much like
Biblical times

The Book of Exodus presents the beginnings of the
Habiru's 'history' as they have recorded it. Rather
than the Book of Genesis, Exodus is for the Hebrews
the Bible's first significant Book. It gives the story of
Moses under whose leadership a motley group of
ethnically different people begins to take on a
specifically 'historic' identity.

Remembering the status of the Habiru as slaves in Egypt (c 1300BC), they were scarcely in such an advanced position as to devise rules for themselves: unless Moses saw himself as an early version of Spartacus. Naturally, they were bound to assimilate those rules that were already in existence.

It cannot be a mere coincidence that the Ten Commandments, almost word for word, parallels the Code of Hammurabi, an Amorite chieftain (1728 – 1686BC). His is not the only Code to have survived from that period. Though some were more extensive than Hammurabi's, they all followed the same principles.

Long before this crowd of different ethnic groups emerged as a Nation, and long before they were made aware that they were God's chosen people, the 'Habiru' like their more civilized hosts, were already living by this set of man-made Laws. As we saw in the section on Myth, Religion always played an enormous part in the lives of peoples who had gods for every eventuality.

It would take many hundreds of years for the Habiru to accept that there was only one God – and that this God had chosen them to be His People, or that it was actually *His* Law that they were expected to keep. This did not really begin to catch on until the times of the Prophets, who told them that their God had made a Promise to their Patriarch, Abraham, and to his descendants. . . and that this meant *them*! Being the beneficiaries of this God-given Pact, they needed a Code of Behaviour, which they would begin to recognize as also being God-given.

Like all codes, it brings with it appropriate sanctions, to ensure that it is kept. However, this particular Law was promulgated, not just to ensure that the people conformed, but also to promote the Promise that those who were faithful to it would inherit God-given rewards.

Moses had always been their traditional law-giver, and it was Moses who declared that this was the Law of God, since when it has been known as the 'Ten Commandments' – the Decalogue.

The Rules governing other national systems held no interest for Old Testament writers. These, had they even remembered it, would have gained nothing by mentioning that the Decalogue was originally Hammurabi's. Even supposing that by the time of writing, no memory of how they originated had survived, it would have served no purpose to mention that this man-made Code had merely been adjusted by the addition of a short prologue consisting of three specifically Hebrew religious precepts.

But it was not until Ezra produced his definitive list of Commands that Jews, in general, would begin to see the Decalogue as the Law of the one true God. This would have been at a time when their religious perspective had begun to see God's hand actually at work in the ways of Man. But the concept that the Law was actually the 'Word of God' did not appear until the time of the Prophets.

THE TEN COMMANDMENTS –
THE DECALOGUE (Exodus 20: 3-17 & 20)

These commandments were given to a frightened people in order 'to keep them from sinning'. The following is a digest:

1. You shall have no gods except me.
2. You shall not take God's name (Yahweh) in vain.
3. Remember to keep the Sabbath day holy.
4. Honour your father and mother.
5   You shall not kill.
6. You shall not commit adultery.
7. You shall not steal.
8. You shall not bear false witness.
9. You shall not covet your neighbour's wife.
10. You shall not covet your neighbour's goods.

Sociology tells us that there is no sense in promulgating a set of Laws where none has ever existed. Where no one knows what Law is, there can be no meaning in 'commitment to keep it'. The problem that exercised the redactors (editors) of the Pentateuch, was that, since there was no tradition that God gave the Law to *Abraham*, where then would be the most adventitious place in the Bible to introduce the Decalogue? [All they had were the two traditions: that the Commandments were given on Mount Sinai or on Mount Horeb.]

'TIMING' WAS THE KEY FOR THE DECALOGUE

There is nothing to prevent us speculating on some options that might have been considered:

Why not introduce God's Law to Adam? That would

certainly make sense not only of the punishment imposed on Cain but would also provide grounds to justify the Flood.

Why not introduce God's Law to Noah? That would have coincided with the new start he made.

Why not introduce the Law when God made His Promise to Abraham, or on those occasions when it was repeated to his descendants? But that would presuppose the existence of a community to which it could apply.

A suggested reason why none of these three options would have been satisfactory was the fact, as the editors knew well, that 'myth' and legend had been very important in the relating of their pre-history. It had also been difficult to choose only those myths, which would serve their purpose in composing the origins of this 'one-God' Hebrew people. *On no account, therefore, was there to be any danger that their all-important Law could be mistaken for myth or legend.*

Some other considerations:

1. To introduce such a Law, suddenly, on a mountain, to an ethnically disparate and basically polytheistic group of people is not a particularly wise course to take, especially since there were no facilities to ensure it was kept.

2. To introduce God's Law to the same ethnically disparate group of people while they were in the process of conquering a country or, later still, when they were dividing up the country amongst themselves, is poor man-management.

3. To introduce the Law to govern the behaviour of a settled worshipping community, presupposes an

already existing law, to which the Ten Commandments are merely an addition.

4. To introduce God's Law when the land was settled and the Kings had been established and able to enforce it, and after the Temple had been built for the worshipping community, seems to be the likeliest and safest option.

However, taking all these considerations into account, the final option seems to us now to have been the obvious choice, as subsequent events turned out. A further reason for their choice may well have been the fact that all slaves crave 'freedom', and as escapees, the Habiru would need to know the reason behind the help they had been given.

So their Saga shows that this is when they were told that only one God was responsible for their freedom, and it was this that prompted the promulgation of the Ten Commandments (Exodus 20).

The Prophets insisted that because of their escape they were indebted to this God and an understanding of this indebtedness was to be seen in terms of their being faithful to God's Law. So the Bible shows the returning Habiru bringing this Law with them, and imposing it on the country they were about to conquer.

Of course, nobody really knows the answer to how, when or why. But such harmless speculation may be of help to those interested in this ongoing detection process.

The Sinai/Horeb Experience can be dated between 1300 and 1200BC, but the Ten Commandments as given in Exodus Ch. 20, were not compiled for over another 600 years, nor completed until much later. By then Chapters 21 and 22 included a total of 64 Commandments.[7] Along with these Chapters 5 and 6 of Deuteronomy (dated 620-570BC), and the account in Leviticus (dated from 538BC) contain additional, then up-dated, liturgical rules.

The complex collection of Rules in the Book of Numbers, would not become the Basis of Hebrew Life for 500 years – after the Sinai event. . . and, as for keeping them, apparently, not even then! Apart from all the mythological scenery, Genesis can be seen being composed against a background of the Ten Commandments. The treatment Cain receives for the murder of his brother, for instance, only serves to highlight this approach.

As these Commandments, already in existence for 500 years, were being observed by the civilized nations of the Near East, there is every reason to suppose that, on Mount Sinai, the Habiru saw God blessing these Laws for *them* – to show His support for His own emerging protégé nation.

Exodus 'Continues' in Joshua and Judges

The Book of Joshua could be called, more accurately, 'Exodus Part 2a'. As Moses is the hero of Exodus, his successor, Joshua, is the hero who organized the Conquest of Canaan. The Book of Judges, which could be called 'Exodus Part 2b', relates the exploits of twelve heroes (Judges) who, for a time, liberated the country from Philistine and Canaanite domination.

---

7. Jewish tradition ultimately established 613 Commands, each traditionally said to be derived from the ten given to Moses.

To help to assimilate this modern approach to Exodus, we are reminded that these people, as they became increasingly aware that God had entered into their national life, were starting to pull away from their dependence on 'Myth'. It is also worth noting that the Decalogue was only gradually written into Hebrew traditions. It was not until Ezra's time (c400BC), that the definitive list of Commandments was produced.

The later Books Leviticus, Numbers and Deuteronomy give us clear evidence that some of the Traditions were giving a new approach to the Law. Ezra again was responsible for much of that work too. 'God gave us our Law. The fact that other nations have similar Laws only shows that our God is right!' is the later understanding underlying the Book of Job and many of those Psalms which show the Psalmist giving 'Three cheers for our God!'.

SUMMARY

Those who read the Bible, often comment on 'biblical inconsistency' and its 'contradictions'. But this is probably because they are not aware of the theological agenda, nor the different traditions enshrined in its construction. They even point to 'contradictions', where there are none.

In fact, the other sources show a surprising regard for a 'consistency' more suited to our sophisticated tastes, since the writers seem sometimes to have reworked their materials more carefully later in favour of the larger picture. But even among these, we occasionally find variations on the same theme. [E.g.

The cliffs at Qumran near the Dead Sea

Gen.11:10 gives **'J's'** chronological note, which strangely jars with the numerical sequences that **'P'** has already lovingly worked out in such tedious detail. On the other hand, **'P'** has not even bothered to 'paper-over' the conflicting details in *his* sources.]

At least three of our first writers began to put down what each thought to be important regarding God's beginning the 'Process of Man', once they had found enough material which would prove useful to them. Their work is to be found chiefly throughout the First Five Books of the Old Testament. Other compilers, coming later, would follow their lead and continue their work. Others, even later, appear to have edited, combined and added to them in a process that would cover the next several hundred years.

$$\boxed{12}$$

Old & New Texts & 'The Word of God'

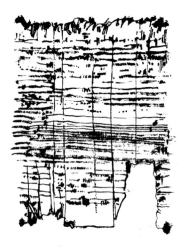

Fragment of a Dead Sea scroll (see cover)

By 135AD 'new' material had been appearing for some sixty years and it was now being copied and distributed. Though it followed the same design as the earlier work (relying heavily on what had gone before), this 'new' material started using updated ideas and, with a fresh approach to the past, it also began to find an 'updated' language.

Authoritative Letters were being circulated. These, too, explained some of the ancient traditions in the light of 'new understandings'. A fresh preaching movement was also evolving. In earlier times this had been the province of wandering prophet-like characters. Now these meditations and sermons were being transcribed, using the Greek material that had been produced in Alexandria during the previous 200 years.

This movement was centred on a character, known as Jesus Christ. For many at that time, this, at last, was the Promised Messiah. His mission was to fulfil all the Hebrew aspirations, to bless their past efforts and to bring them their freedom. But, for the Orthodox Jew, and many others, his inauspicious arrival counted against his being 'kosher'.

It was not possible to prevent the disintegration of treasured time-worn scrolls, so copies, and copies of copies, were circulated – eventually these, too, would be replaced. Remnants of much earlier work were also being copied and either collected or rejected depending on those into whose hands they fell.

Copies of this New Material probably took precedence in the few synagogues where the congregations had become followers of the 'Way' – the name given to this New Movement. Not unreasonably, there were some people who understood this new movement to be a 'replacement' of the old Hebrew traditions. The more Orthodox Jews, who became followers of the 'Way' saw it merely as a 'renewal' of their earlier understandings.

But, as this new teaching took hold of people's minds, it led many to withdraw completely from the old traditions, which Orthodox Jewry had always held so sacred. Apart from the Old Testament material found in the Qumran caves by the Dead Sea, and the Scrolls found at Masada and Hever, there are also Hebrew and Aramaic copies known as the Masoretic Text. With the Syriac versions, there is the Peshita Bible, the Samaritan Pentateuch and also many other collections. We also have the Greek Versions, among which is the Alexandrian Pentateuch which contains Palestinian revisions.

The Bible also appears in various Manuscripts, including the famous Uncial Codices:[8] the Codex Vaticanus, the Codex Sinaiticus, the Codex Alexandrinus, and the Codex Marchalianus. Then come the Latin versions, dating from the fourth century AD. These are translations from the Hebrew, from the Greek and then from a combination of both. Added to this material, there are also the many different copies that exist.

Then non-religious scholars became involved, contributing their own brand of commentary on these writings, including those belonging to a world outside the Hebrew Story, like Pliny and Josephus. These added their historical 'pennyworth', corroborating the Jewish religious developments that began to unfold during the reign of the Emperor Tiberius (14-37AD). Since then the number of translations began to grow. But the number of versions that arose with the discovery of printing is now legion.

---

8. Uncial Codices are composed throughout in upper case script.

Qumran

In 1947 young shepherds poking about in the caves at Qumran, near Jericho, by the Dead Sea, found some pottery that was clearly very old. Mention of it caused great interest. Amongst the breakages, were hundreds of pieces of parchment and papyrus, some still intact, which contained written material. These writings were found to be about 2,000 years old and identified as copies of various Hebrew Biblical books. There were also copies of the Book of Jubilees and the Book of Enoch, neither of which appeared in the Bible.

Archaeologists and scholars decided that these findings were the work of a community of monks that had settled there about 200BC. The caves provided accommodation for men who wished to escape the abuses that had crept into the Jewish way of life. Known as 'Essenes', they maintained a growing community until the Romans destroyed their monastery (c 70AD). At the same time, Masada, the famous Jewish hilltop camp south of the Dead Sea, fell to the Roman siege.

☐

'Creation by word' is an idea that appears in Egyptian thought as early as 2700BC, much earlier than any Old Testament material. For our purposes, the 'Word of God' was an Old Testament expression, and was only used for particular revelations to the Prophets. Although the 'Word of God' is an essential element in the Old Testament conception of 'history', Hebrews, when referring to their sacred books, would use the expression the 'Torah' for the 'Law of God'.

Not until all the works had been collected and, after the Church had decided on those Books that were to be included in the final list, did Christendom describe this collection as the 'Holy Bible'. Local Church councils in North Africa first decided on a list of Books during the fourth century AD. This list was finally accepted at the Council of Trent (Italy) in April 1546. Interestingly enough, it is not official teaching to describe the total contents of the Bible as the 'Word of God'. This is worth noting, as we have discovered (p.19) that several Books contain a considerable amount of material that is clearly not so.

Christendom recognizes the Bible as the 'Word of God', so great sensitivity is required when embarking on this tour. Your Guide, like the rest of the visiting party to the castle, has come upon it very late in the day. Though part of our heritage, the Bible only belongs to us as successors to the Hebrews. They were the first to realize the revelation contained in its origins, and they were the first to write it down.

HOW MUCH IS EXPLANATION?

The question still remains: How much of the Bible is 'Word of God' and how much is not? Was the Revelation written down first, or did some explanation precede it? We know the traditions pre-existed any 'Word from God' – and we know that 'myth' came before anything else! But how much 'explanation' was later added to the original Scripture? *Good question!*

The Hebrew national Tradition begins with God giving the Law to Moses (Exodus). However, this tradition is passed down to succeeding generations both in an oral as well as in a written fashion; and in order to assist the memory, and to avoid mistakes, the oral traditions got themselves included in the writing.

The composition of the Bible used many different literary devices. Along with these we find 'Revelation' in the form of a Midrash (a word for 'that which explains the background' against which a particular story is written). Then there are the Oral, ('word of mouth') traditions, which are found in the 'Halacha', 'Mishnah', 'Gemara' and in the 'Talmud'.

The 'Talmud' is better known because it is more recent, but all four traditions explain, in their own way, the gradual development and expansion of the Hebrew Law. The 'Stories', linking the pieces of Revelation together, come down to us in the 'Haggadah'.

It is worth remembering that the Bible is the Hebrew understanding of Hebrew development as it evolved under God's protection. The notion that the Hebrew Bible is the 'Word of God' only arose after the whole Bible, with its two Testaments (New and Old), had been completed and had been accepted by Christendom as an 'unalterable rule of life'. But, as we have seen, despite its description as the 'Word of God', it contains a lot that is not.

What's In a Name?

Since the Old Testament Books originally had no names or titles, let alone Chapters and Verses, it is easy to see how some oral traditions could be copied alongside the original texts. Not only that – some were put in the wrong places; and/or added to the text for no other reason than to cut down the work of having to write them out again separately!

SUMMARY

We now have a clearer picture of the way in which the Hebrews developed and then collected their writings. After translation, these received their names, and later still were given numbered chapters and verses. In the fullness of time they got printed. Obviously, the approach taken here will be more advanced than that which is found in School text-books.

This *Guide* has attempted to trace briefly the development of the Bible, from its earliest beginnings. It should not be difficult to realize that people living 3,000 years ago had a completely different way of looking at things, and that therefore the manner of their descriptions would differ considerably from any modern understanding. In addition, Near Eastern people had different languages, different cultures and backgrounds and were then only just beginning to discover what civilization might have in store for them.

The Hazan cave, Israel, showing dwellings from the Roman period

Appendix

The Books of the Bible

The Bible can be seen as a Library of different Books, provided we remember that roughly similar theological themes run through each. The differences between the Books, becomes clearer as we learn more of the origins and background of the Hebrews. The table of Contents in your Bible lists the Books according to their position in the chronological position in the development of this people. The list given here follows the suggested order in which they were composed and gives approximate dates for each Book with a little about the writers, contents and their context. Note: All dates given for the Old Testament are BC.

OLD TESTAMENT

THE PENTATEUCH (the First Five Books), initiated in the tenth century, provides a 'chronological' narrative with additional expositions, meditations and connecting passages. What we have here is the result of considerable work that took some 600 years to develop.

Exodus opens with preparations for an Escape of the Egyptian slaves, which then becomes their most important religious truth. Over the next 2,000 years, this theme of 'deliverance from oppression' gradually consumed the whole of Western religious thinking. Rules, introduced to keep the minds of the people on what God had done, include some preliminary legislation regarding religious ritual.

Leviticus gives rules for religious ritual in greater detail, especially those concerning 'sacrifice'.

Numbers then adds the rules governing social behaviour. Those incidents of popular rebellion, not found in Exodus, are related here. Genesis was also being constructed during this time.

Genesis covers several primitive aspects of God, namely His Sovereignty, Holiness, Justice and Mercy, which are built into a number of Creation Stories. God issues a Promise to which the conditions (in Exodus) are later attached. The whole work relies largely on foreign folklore.

Deuteronomy – 'the second law' – recalls God's Promise to Abraham in terms of the up-dated thinking of the sixth century BC. It is Deuteronomy's treatment of the 'deliverance' episode that gets quoted in the New Testament. Deuteronomy is second only in importance to Exodus in the formation of the Pentateuch.

THE HISTORICAL BOOKS

Book of Ruth. (c900) Ruth, David's great grandmother, was a Moabite slave employed by Boaz, a distant cousin. Even then the Hebrews need to be reminded that they began as slaves, and that are not as *exclusively* God's people as they had thought. Concerned with lineage, it contains the first story of a 'king' – Elimelech.

Book of Judges is a set of tribal stories, which include the Sichem Accord. First edited in the eighth century, it is an embarrassing record of Hebrew infidelity, when each did as he pleased.

Book of Joshua relating eleventh-century events, was still being reworked in the sixth century. It continues the story of Exodus by charting the invasion of Canaan and its eventual conquest and settlement.

First Book of Kings (c550) tells of the 'kingdom' and starts with Saul (c1020). The Prophets encouraged religious observance, but, later, lacking appropriate support from the kings, they preached in vain.

Second Book of Kings (c550) continues the exploits of the

Prophets, who supplanted the Kings. These two Books, initially called 'Former' and 'Latter' Prophets, were given their present names much later.

Clearly the work of more than one person, the **Book of Samuel**, was completed in the sixth century. It was later divided into two Books. The Talmud says Samuel composed it, but then who is the character whose death is noted in 1 Sam.25? It is more likely that the famous name 'Samuel' was used to give provenance to a collection of literary pieces that, over a period of about 200 years, were gathered together and worked on by several different writers.

Ezra (c400) tells of the rebuilding of Solomon's Temple, built between c955-948 but destroyed in 586. Since the Jews understood their traditions in terms of the Law, Ezra codified this Law. Ezra is the author most likely to have been responsible for the final draft of Deuteronomy.

Nehemiah (c400) details the rebuilding of the city walls of Jerusalem and the resettlement of Judah during the period after the People had returned from Exile in 538.

First Book of Chronicles (completed c300) was composed after the Books of Kings and Samuel had been completed. The first Book begins with Adam and describes Hebrew religious history – but from the Priests' point of view.

Second Book of Chronicles, also completed c300 and quite different from the Books of Kings and Samuel. It continues the Priests' Story, finishing with the Decree of Cyrus II, and his successor, Darius, who returned the exiled Jews to their homeland (538).

Tobit (c200), not in the Hebrew Bible, reflects the contemporary religious situation. In the absence of Prophets, this story attempts to edify its hearers at a time when God seems to have abandoned his people.

Judith (c150) weaves together some widely separated facts in Israel's history in order to show God's providence in restoring everything. It is yet another exposition of the Exodus/Judges experience.

Second Book of Maccabees (c124) is largely the work of one, Jason of Cyrene. Letters in the Temple archives provided much of his material. Later, this was severely edited. It also contains the earliest Biblical reference to the doctrine of the 'resurrection from the dead'.

Esther (completed by 114) reflects facts during the Babylonian Exile and dates from Ezra's time. It relates an escape (annually recalled at the Jewish Feast: 'Purim' in Feb/March) and illustrates God's gracious protection while reflecting contemporary anti-Semitic pogroms as well as the slaughter of Gentiles.

First Book of Maccabees. Completed in c63, the author's identity is unknown. Like Chronicles (to which it may be a sequel) it deals with the difficult times during the Seleucid period as the Book of Chronicles deals with the Persian Empire. The Maccabean Revolt (160s) won the Jews independence and increased their territory. Their approach to contemporary history shows the author and editors to be strongly nationalistic in their sympathies.

THE WISDOM BOOKS

The Song of Songs, usually taken to be a tenth-century collection, is a moving drama about human love. The purpose for its inclusion in the Bible, however, has puzzled scholars for centuries.

Book of Proverbs (eighth century with later additions) is a collection of warnings, coupled with such secular and religious considerations on Hebrew history, as affected Jewish everyday life. It is an anthology of earlier collections attributed to Solomon who also used many Egyptian ideas to instruct his people. However, most of these observations are more likely to have reached their present form at the end of the fifth century BC.

Job (between 600-450) is a masterpiece of allegorical writing. It attempts to answer the problem of pain and undeserved suffering, while acknowledging Job's limited ability to comprehend it.

Ecclesiastes – called 'Koheleth' or written by someone of that name (fourth or third century) offers a generally pessimistic view of life to Jews if they live it without putting God first.

Psalms (finalized c385AD) is a collection of ancient Hymns. Its divine praises, its meditations on subsequent Hebrew religious history and its cries of despair, makes it a marvellous and powerful anthology.

A teacher and one-time diplomat, Sirach wrote **Ecclesiasticus** (c180). By showing that true wisdom is to be found in Israel, this is really a defence against the challenge of the new Greek thinking.

Wisdom, once thought to be from the third century AD, it is probably by a Greek in Alexandria sometime before 100BC. Even though Chapters 11-19 emphasize Egypt's contact with Israel in Solomon's time, it is now thought unlikely to have been composed by him.

THE PROPHETS

This is a Collection of those works of the Prophets that have survived. It was not generally accepted as a collection of 'sacred books' until the end of the second century BC.

Isaiah contains three separate works, from between c783-c510. Each examines three specific stages in Hebrew history. The manner of writing shows that each section has been edited and re-interpreted by disciples. It was normal for copyists, working in writing Schools, to be engaged in this sort of work. [Chapters 1-39 (750-c700); Chapters 40-55 (c550); Chapters 56-66 (after 515)]

Amos (c760), the best known of the Minor Prophets, was a shepherd from the South. He went to Samaria to try (in vain) to recall the northern tribes to the practice of their religion.

Like Amos, **Hosea** (between 750-732) saw the return of his wife as a presage of the return of the unfaithful northern tribes before the Assyrian invasion of 721, but it was not!

Micah (between 742-687) came from southern peasant stock. He was shocked by the overt injustice of the degenerate rich despite the general poverty of the common people.

Zephaniah (c640-609) played a significant part in King Josiah's desire for a reformation, after the disastrous reign of Manasseh who, preferring the magic of wizards, silenced all the prophets.

Jeremiah (627-598) is one of the outstanding personalities in the Bible. While the Jews had generally slid back into moral apathy, he remonstrated against their rank injustice by pointing out their religious potential.

Nahum (c615). Assyria, then the 'most brutal of empire builders', fell to Babylon in 612. Nahum persuaded their people to change their lives – but his warnings came too late.

Habakkuk (between 605-597), contemporary with Jeremiah, was exasperated with the constant economic prosperity of the wicked while the righteous continued to suffer privation.

Lamentations (early sixth century) is a series of dirges, in which Jeremiah reflects on the destruction of Jerusalem in 586. He entitled each section with a letter from the Hebrew alphabet.

Baruch contains several different sections, possibly by different authors and is thought to have been compiled between 597-538. Originally a Hebrew work, it contains later additions in Greek.

Ezekiel (c593-568) was another outstanding personality. From about 587 onwards, this priest, visionary and missionary went to Babylon to minister to the Jews who were exiled there.

Haggai and **Zechariah** (c520). Having recently returned from Exile, the people are understandably more interested in building up their material interests than in the religious and moral aspects of their lives. To demonstrate God's goodness, both Haggai and Zechariah highlighted their past good fortune to encourage their people to see the rebuilding of their Temple as their first priority.

Joel (c400) preached a message for all time: 'While He must punish sin, God always pleads with sinners, longing to pardon those who genuinely turn from their evil ways.'

Obadiah (mid-fifth century) was probably the only prophet to preach to those who had been left behind in Judah in the early years of the exile. His work is the shortest of all the prophetic scrolls.

Malachi (mid-fifth century). His message was: Since God never changes, the now religiously indifferent people must be consistent in keeping the Law if they are to reap its benefits.

Jonah (between 400-200) Jonah was always identified with the one mentioned in 2 Kgs.14:25. (dated c550) However, this work uses words that are only found in *later* Hebrew literature. The writer first rebels against having to preach in Nineveh. He is further put out when the pagan Ninevites actually take him seriously, while the Jews back home do not!

Daniel, (composed c165) uses excerpts of the Hebrew Story not only to show that God is in full control, but that Providence caters as much for the individual as it does for great nations.

NEW TESTAMENT

Just as no Old Testament writer was commissioned to compose any literature, neither was any so commissioned to write for the New Testament. Similarly, none of these works are the accounts of eye-witnesses, but were composed later by writers using oral and written traditions that were already well known.

The Gospels appear to be a series of collected sermons, or memories of sermons and contemporary meditations addressed to different groups of people. As such they were linked together with sufficient narrative to place them in a given time and place. Each has its own agenda, though it will be clear that **Mark** will have used some material that was used by **Matthew**. **Luke** also used some of it, but he had recourse to other traditions as well – but traditions not known to Matthew or Mark. Though the Gospel writers had access to similar oral and written material, it is unlikely that the editors of one particular tradition, say Matthew's, were aware of what details were being used by the others. There is little evidence that there was any collusion between them.

Like the Old Testament Story, which really began with the central event in Hebrew History (Exodus), the New Testament begins with the extraordinary event of the Resurrection. This provided Christ's followers with an incentive to write about it. The New Testament traces their attempt to do so. 'Testament' is the word Tertullian chose for 'Covenant' as he saw the New Testament fulfilling the role of Epilogue to the whole collection of the Biblical Library. However, another point of view makes this 'Epilogue' the springboard from which Christendom develops from its Jewish roots.

The New Testament gives the Story of the Messiah who is seen, by Christendom, to fulfil all those Jewish aspirations. But in so doing, the Messiah, the Christ, goes far beyond what was an exclusively Jewish agenda. The earliest material, that considered the Christ to be the development of Jewish aspirations, are thought to be **Paul's Letters to the Thessalonians**. While the bulk of the Letters attributed to Paul were written between 57-70, several are more likely to have been written later by his disciples. Though Paul refers to his work as 'gospel' material, the Four Gospels are later works. Known as 'Evangelists', the four Gospel writers produced works that are listed first in the New Testament, since it was realized that their awareness of the 'Christ' phenomenon – which must have been a most extraordinary experience – was to be a new beginning for their Jewish readers. Like the writers of earlier Biblical works, each had his own agenda.

The traditional way of referring to a Gospel is 'the Gospel according to St Mark' or 'according to Matthew'. This means that it is written in accordance with Mark's, or Matthew's tradition. Scholars are at last convinced that none of the Gospels can possibly be eye-witness accounts. In this regard, their work is consistent with the traditions of their predecessors, in that the Gospels are a series of meditations and sermons, linked by narrative. They are all based on oral traditions and were composed to point out, as the eventual editors saw it, the role Christ played in the continuing development of the Hebrew Saga. The works were compiled in accordance with traditions that had become associated with the following persons:

Mark (between 65-70) approaches his account of the Christ from the understanding that nothing worthwhile can be achieved except through the 'suffering of hopelessness'. So he ends his story with Christ's ignominious execution. Curiously, his story seems to show that, besides himself, only the 'demons' actually know 'who' the Christ is!

On the other hand, **Matthew**'s story, composed during the 70s, is driven by the unassailable fact that Christ is the Holy One of God who has come to fulfil all the Hebrew expectations. Everyone (with the notable exception of the

Temple authorities) realizes that Christ acts and speaks with a unique 'authority'. Matthew describes Christ as the King and consistently points out that Christ's words and actions actually fulfil the ancient Jewish prophecies.

John (between 90-100), using much material known to the other Gospel writers, actually provides a different outlook on the 'Christ' phenomenon. This Gospel sees Christ, as God-the-Son who pre-existed the Creation. Coming from 'eternity', he consistently shows foreknowledge of all situations in which he is involved. All that is now necessary is that his readers should realize that the Father had sent Him, the Son, to tell the world that everyone is a Child of God.

Luke, on the contrary, goes beyond this. Though he never met Christ, some of his writers may well have done so. His work corroborates the other Gospels. Writing between 70-85, he describes Christ, the Man, and uses Christ's 'life story' as an introduction to what follows. Like Matthew and Mark, Luke heralds the coming of the Holy Spirit, whose story he describes in the Acts of the Apostles.

Paul, who does not appear on the missionary scene until after the Gospel events are finished, is introduced in **Acts of the Apostles**, as the Apostle of the Holy Spirit. Paul, like John later, wrote to those different 'young community churches' that he had established during his travels. The addressees are usually named in the titles. Those other Letters, which are included in the Biblical Library, are of a more general application and were compiled between 62-90. They were attributed to other disciples.

2 Peter is now thought to have been written by a disciple early in the second century AD.

The Book of Revelations (also known as Apocalypse) (90-96) is attributed to John and brings the New Testament to a close. This is a composite document; it is not certain which 'John' was ultimately responsible for it. It is a series of Christian reflections on Old Testament themes.

It is not an easy Book to comprehend, though the central theme is clear: 'the Almighty One reigns'. Every reader is reminded of God's eternal sovereignty, Christ's eternal victory (over evil). The danger of taking it literally, is apparent when one realizes that it is written in coded symbols.

To any second-century Roman official finding such a work, which to us clearly depicts the triumph of the Church along with the collapse of the Empire, it would have seemed particularly subversive; for which the severest penalties were reserved. Even those now 'in the know' do not usually see it in these terms. But to those who recognize its references to Hebrew lore and Jewish symbolism, its triumphant message regarding the Church is crystal clear.

'Revelation' uses Old Testament material to support an understanding that, not only has everything contained in the Bible now been completed but also that all its prophecies have already been fulfilled.

By now, readers may well be asking: What next? That is another good question. For an attempt at an answer we move beyond the Bible – to the Church.

Bibliography

Jerusalem Bible. (1974) Darton Longman & Todd
The Jerome Biblical Commentary. (1980) Geoffrey Chapman
Vawter, Bruce (1977) *On Genesis*. Geoffrey Chapman
Hauret, Charles (1964) *Beginnings – Genesis and Modern
Science*. Priory Press, Chicago
Haade, Eugene OFM (1981) *Guide to the Holy Land*.
Franciscan Press, Jerusalem
New Larousse Encyclopaedia of Mythology (1974). Hamlyn
Publishing Co., London
Enchiridion Symbolorum (1957). Herder, Rome
Staniforth, M. (trans) (1981) *Early Christian Writings*. Penguin
Documents of the Christian Church (1959). Henry Bettenson
World's Classics
Brown, Raymond E. (1993) *Bible Guide*. Harper Collins,
Glasgow

Recommended Reading

Goldberg & Rayner (1987) *The Jewish People, their History and
Religion*. Penguin
de Chardin, Teillard (1955) *The Phenomenon of Man*
A Popular Presentation of Catholic Belief (1996) Redemptorist
Publications, Hampshire
Charpentier, Etienne (1982) *How to read the Old Testament*.
SCM Press, London
Charpentier, Etienne (1982) *How to read the New Testament*.
SCM Press, London
Brown, R.E. (1985) *Biblical Exegesis & Church Doctrine*.
London
Megiven, J.J. (ed) (1978) *Official Catholic Teachings: Bible
Interpretation*. Consortium Book; Wilmington, NC
Kung, Hans (1977) *On being a Christian*. Collins
Brown, Raymond E. (1985) *Biblical Exegesis and Church
Doctrine*. Geoffrey Chapman
Brown, Raymond E. (1990) *Responses to 101 Questions on the
Bible*. Paulist Press, New York

Index